CW00545917

Thomas Plunkett of the 95th Rifles.

Hero, Villain:
Fact or Fiction

Ken Trotman Publishing

Published in 2010 by Ken Trotman Publishing.
Booksellers & Publishers
P.O.Box 505
Godmanchester
Huntingdon PE29 2XW
England
Tel: 01480 454292
Fax: 01480 384651
www.Kentrotman.com

ISBN 978-1-907417-03-0

To my wife Barbara

Printed in Great Britain by the MPG Books Group,
Bodmin and King's Lynn

Introduction

The 95th Rifles have become an even more recognisable and popular regiment around the world since the introduction of Richard Sharpe, the creation of author Bernard Cornwell. Since when he has been transferred to the small screen and brought to life by the actor Sean Bean. The television series has been a great recruiting campaign for the regiment; though it has caused a myth to evolve around the 95th Rifles, some of which should be challenged before creeping into future history as fact. It is to stop such claims reaching that stage that I have embarked on a series of research articles that will help dispel such fabrications. I started by tackling a subject already entrenched in Regimental lore which often forms the basis of claims about the accuracy of the arm used by the regiment in its early years, the 'Baker Rifle.' I hope students of the period will find this book informative and make them want to take this research further, while not forgetting, that at some period, new documentation or artefacts can emerge to alter one's thinking.

George Caldwell

George and the Rifles

George Caldwell is probably better known for his partnership with Robert Cooper as co-author of the Rifle Green series, gaining much success and credit as serious researchers. Their association has since been complemented by the paintings and sketches of the artist James Dann, who consented to illustrate the text for this work. George has been researching the 95th Rifles/The Rifle Brigade for over forty years, his interest fired when joining the Rifle Brigade/3rd Green Jackets as a band boy in January 1963. This research however lies outside of the normal remit of the Rifle Green series therefore George was able to offer the research on Thomas Plunkett in this format in a first time collaboration with Richard Brown, of Ken Trotman Publishing.

George's knowledge of the regiment is considered to be exceptional for the period covering the Peninsula and Waterloo periods, extending to Victorian Britain, making him respected within the regimental system. George has been consulted by many historians and authors over the years to help clarify or extend many points with which they have found difficulty. When the regiment celebrated its 200th Centenary in Winchester in 2000 the museum produced a commemorative booklet giving a short but overall view of the regiment's deeds and accomplishments including the unique record of 27 Victoria Crosses awarded, with the rider, 'How many regiments could count among their alumni, and all in office within the bracket of a few years, a Lord Chancellor, a Chairman of the Bar Council and President of the law Society?' The quota of authors, historical and otherwise, is very considerable. Nor was this exceptional talent limited to the officers of the Regiment. The special quality of the Riflemen, NCO's and Warrant Officers is illustrated by the number of well-known authors the regiment produced from the ranks (*including in recent years ex-Bandsman Caldwell*)...a fine and lasting tribute to such a dedicated Regimental author. George has a special affinity with the Bands and Bandmasters of the regiment and is possibly the leading authority on the subject having researched all aspects of their progression from the raising of the regiment in 1800 through to 1965, when the Rifle Brigade became the 3rd Battalion Royal Green Jackets, now part of the new Regiment, 'The Rifles.'

George's research continues with a passion, his goal, to produce the ultimate range of historical fact-based books on the regiment, giving future historians an in-depth series of publications to consult, taking Rifles history to another level. The books and articles completed to date with Robert Cooper are already the envy of many a regimental archive. George has lived on the Island of Anglesey for the last 30 years with his wife Barbara who helps with research and the typing of his manuscripts. Joining, when the occasion arises with Robert and Carol Cooper and James Dann they represent a formidable team, of which the Rifles should be truly proud.

Acknowledgements

My special thanks go to Barabara Caldwell for her constant support and for converting my long hand manuscripts into a legible format; to Carol Cooper for keeping me within the bounds of the English language and Robert Cooper for his assistance with research; James Dann for his willingness to enhance the text of this book; Allan Lagden for his research in Colchester; Judith Farrington for her impeccable research knowledge of The National Archives; Philip Haythornthwaite for his invaluable help and expertise; Major Ron Cassidy and Major Ken Gray of the Rifles museum and archives for their assistance and help with material for this book; Roy and Sandra Strange for all their help in Chichester and providing me internet notes on Plunkett; Richard Brown for his willingness to undertake this new challenge.

Thomas Plunkett of the 95th Rifles

Hero, Villain: Fact or Fiction.

Over many years of researching the history of the 95th Rifles/The Rifle Brigade, one Rifleman's name comes to the fore more than any other, 'Thomas Plunkett', whose main claim to fame was his remarkable ability with the rifle. A famous incident on the retreat to Corunna during the winter of 1808-09, when he shot and killed the distinguished French cavalry General, Colbert, reserved him his place in our regimental history and hall of fame.

However, having examined all the written evidence surrounding this incident it is quite clear most of what has been said or written about this particular feat of arms has been passed down in its present form solely from hearsay evidence. This has now become firmly entrenched in the regimental history and, as far as I am aware never been challenged? Most of what we know about Plunkett's service in the 95th comes from the colourful memoirs of another well known Rifleman, Edward Costello - a fellow Irishman - written in all fairness many years after the events, when those of a certain age will agree facts can become a little distorted. The reason for this in-depth look at the man and his claim to fame is to strip away the myth and legend that has grown up around Plunkett and expose the bare facts. To achieve this it was necessary to start with a blank canvas to build up a picture of him from scratch. Throughout the whole of my research I have only come across one original account for the period covering Plunkett's shooting of Colbert, this from the pen of a fellow Rifleman, Captain George Miller. His account has been around since 1842. Historians such as Sir William Cope have used parts of it but up until now the identity of the writer has never been known. The same source remarkably also gives us a personal insight into Plunkett's ability with the rifle and the working relationship he established with his Captain. Miller is the only person, as far as I am aware, to leave details of Plunkett's notoriety in the South American Campaign of 1807 and on the memorable retreat to Corunna, 1808-09.

Before going any further in establishing my case surrounding Plunkett's shooting of General Colbert, it is essential to prove Thomas Plunkett existed and what is more important if he actually served in the 95th Rifles. To do this I had to consult The National Archives (TNA) formerly the Public Records Office (PRO). The first thing the reader will notice is that I refer to Plunkett with a double 't' the general consensus in the archive documents is to spell his name this way. I traced two Thomas Plunkett's in the pension discharge (WO/120/30) documents in the ranks of the 95th Rifles during the Peninsula and Waterloo periods. These two Riflemen were then checked against the muster/pay-list rolls in the WO 12 series, for the whole of the Rifles/Rifle Brigade[1], from these it is quite clear that only one can be the Thomas Plunkett described by Captain Miller and the subject of this research. The second Thomas Plunkett of the pension list is only ever shown in the musters with the Christian name 'John'. He served in the 3rd Battalion 95th, and took part in the Battle of Barrosa. Therefore, he cannot be confused with Thomas Plunkett of Corunna. To clarify this point I have transcribed both men's pension details below:

---

[1] The 95th were taken out of the line in 1816 and re-styled the Rifle Brigade, for their services at Waterloo.

1) The eliminated Thomas Plunkett:

Born: Glen Hough, Antrim. Discharged 4th October 1816 aged 43 years, total length of service 12 years and two months. Received a pension of six pence per day, due to gunshot wounds to left leg, right leg, and left arm. He served in No 4 Company at Barrosa; Ciudad Rodrigo; Badajoz; and Salamanca all in 3/95th, also shown as having service in the 2nd Garrison Company, this probably after being wounded and waiting for final discharge. He was not at Waterloo, an important factor in establishing the right Thomas Plunkett.

2) Thomas Plunkett, the subject of this research:

Born Newtown, Wexford, trade given as a labourer; height 5 feet 6 inches; hair brown, eyes grey, with a pallid complexion. He enlisted Dublin 10th May 1805 in the 95th Rifles, he also had further service of two years with the 41st Regiment Foot, and two years six months, plus another three years, in Militia and Veterans' battalions. His service in the 95th was twelve years six months. He was also entitled to an extra two years towards his pension as was every man who fought at Waterloo, bringing his total length of service to twenty years which confirms the above figures. Thomas Plunkett was discharged November-December 1817 aged thirty four[2], receiving a pension of one shilling per day[3]. The reason stated for his

---

[2] In 1832 when Plunkett commuted his pension he would have been 49 years of age.

[3] Edward Costello says in his memoirs that Plunkett received only 6d per day pension. The only way he would have known the amount awarded to Plunkett is if he had told him, this would have to have been after his return from Canada around 1833-34. Therefore, if Tom told him he received this

discharge, "worn-out".

Thomas Plunkett enlisted into the 2nd Battalion 95th Rifles on the 10th May 1805; though the Waterloo musters give his enlistment date as 8th May. Sometimes the difference on enlistment can be attributed to either the date of joining or the actual day legally sworn in by a magistrate. The 2nd Battalion 95th Rifles had only been formed in 1805; Plunkett therefore would have been one of the volunteers or recruits for the new battalion. He was posted into Captain Bennett's company then stationed at Canterbury, before marching to Brabourne Lees. A number of Riflemen and Non-Commissioned Officers were transferred into the 2nd Battalion, to give it some back-bone. As a result, the 1st Battalion became under strength. On the 25th June 1805 Plunkett, along with a number of Riflemen transferred from the 2nd Battalion into the 1st Battalion. The muster quarter for September to December of that year shows him as being stationed at Bexhill and Deal. The end of December 1805 to March 1806 he is once again shown in Captain Bennett's company, therefore this officer must also have transferred from the 2nd Battalion. The 1st Battalion was now stationed at Lowestoft and Woodbridge. From March to June 1806 Plunkett is at Colchester and Ospringe. By this time he was an experienced Rifleman and had developed into an expert shot with the rifle. The process a recruit went through to master the rifle at this time is worth noting here. They were first instructed in the art of loading and firing the rifle when in close order with cartridges. When a more deliberate aim was required, they were taught to load with powder and loose ball. The distance used for the recruit when first being taught to fire

---

lesser amount then we can be sure he was being economical with the truth!

the rifle was set at sixty to ninety yards without the use of a rest. As they progressed and became more proficient at this distance it was gradually increased by degrees from ninety to three hundred yards. Once they were skilful at the latter distance the recruit was taught to fire resting on one knee, lying on their back and stomach, then every other position required by a Rifleman. Plunkett must have adapted quite easily to these drills for he was soon established as a marksman. With this distinction as a 3rd class shot to his name he would have been entitled to wear a green cockade in his shako above the regulation black leather one. A white cockade would have denoted he was a second class shot. Those with only the black cockade were basic or first class shots.

In 1806, Plunkett's company formed part of the Expedition under Brigadier Robert Craufurd bound for South America, to reinforce General Whitelock. Three companies of the 2nd Battalion 95th Rifles under the command of Major Robert Travers had already taken part in the successful attack on Monte Video which took place on the 3rd February 1807, while the five 1st Battalion companies were still at sea, eventually arriving towards the end of May that same year. The plan now was to attack Buenos Aires for the second time, having already captured and lost it once before! However the Spanish General Liniers was more than prepared to meet this stronger British force. He had placed his guns so as to cover the streets along which he thought the British would advance; others he placed so they could provide a flanking fire. Trenches were cut, and houses barricaded and provided with all kinds of missiles to be thrown down upon the attackers. The houses of Buenos Aires were flat-topped dwellings which had been palisaded, turning each roof top into a mini fort. At his disposal were 9000 soldiers and 6000 irregulars of varying quality with which to defend the town. Five thousand of his best marksmen were posted amongst the houses with ample provisions and ammunition. A further two thousand occupied the Bull-Ring and the remainder he placed in the fort and various strong positions of defence.

The initial advance on the 2nd July 1807 was successful; Craufurd defeated and routed the Spanish force that opposed his column at the Corral. The following day the British continued the advance on the town and fort in thirteen separate columns, while the 38th and 45th Regiments made individual flanking movements against the Bull-Ring and the Residencia. However, General Whitelock's orders were written in such a manner that caused confusion amongst the commanders of the columns. Craufurd's force advanced in two separate columns with the Rifle companies of the 95th split between each unit. Craufurd's account of what took place in his advance is confirmed by the evidence given at Whitelock's Court Martial. Craufurd's columns met with little resistance until nearing the town and reaching the area close to the river. The left column under the command of Lieutenant Colonel Pack of the 71st Regiment came up against severe opposition in the streets leading to the market place. This division split into two separate units in an attempt to reach the Jesuits' College and attack the defenders to avoid the mounting casualties they were receiving. As a result, the half-column under Lieutenant Colonel Cadogan with Major Travers of the 95th were forced to take shelter in an inappropriate building and having been completely surrounded were forced to surrender. Craufurd was eventually reunited with the other half column under Pack, and made a defensive stand at the Convent of St Domingo, from where they could hear the firing in the town gradually diminishing, except for around the convent. Craufurd says, "Between eleven and twelve o'clock, a Spanish officer with a *flag of truce* (my italics) came to the convent sent by General Liniers, who informed me that our attacks had failed, that the 88th Regiment and many others were prisoners and to summon me to surrender to which I gave the most peremport (sic) refusal." It was clear to Craufurd now that his force was the only one remaining within the town and being close to the centre were completely cut off by the large Spanish force, which swelled as the other units surrendered. Craufurd continues, "Nothing now remained possible but to confine ourselves to the defence of the convent and this defence consisted chiefly in the fire of the Riflemen from the top which was extremely well managed by Major Mcleod, but after some time the quantity of round-shot, grape and musketry to which they were exposed was so great as to force them to quit the only situations from whence our fire could prevent the further approach of the enemy's cannon towards the side of it which was near to the market and the whole of which front consisted only of wooden gates. After maintaining the post till four o'clock I was of the opinion that a retreat, surrounded as we were in every direction by six or seven thousand men with many guns occupying all the houses and street; that the enemy had it perfectly in his power to annihilate the detachment if we continued there till midnight set in. After consulting with Lieutenant Colonel's Pack and Guard and Major Mcleod I felt it my duty to communicate with the enemy by holding out a flag of truce and surrender the brigade as prisoners of war." It is during this period of street fighting and the defence of the convent that Thomas Plunkett is first brought to our attention, establishing his prowess with the rifle.

The muster rolls incidentally for this period 25th June to 24th September 1806 still show him in Captain Bennett's company but now on board the armed transport *Chapman*, then from the

25th December 1806 until the 14th March 1807 still with Captain Bennett onboard the transports, *Chapman* or *Alexander*. From 25th March to 24th June 1807 again on board the transports *Hero* and *Alexander*, finally the last two musters covering the period 25th June to the 24th December 1807 on board the same transports, until returning to Colchester, England, December 1808. The musters, as we can clearly see give no indication as to him or any other Riflemen ever having landed in South America, though we know this was the case. The regimental history and Captain Miller state that Plunkett and Fisher were called for and hoisted onto the flat roof of a low building adjoining the convent. Plunkett and Fisher's position commanded the principal street leading to this part of the city.

From here these two Riflemen (obviously chosen for their skill with the rifle) put a continuous and telling fire into the enemy. They kept this up for a number of hours being supplied with ammunition from their comrades below while all the time they were also receiving a heavy return of fire, in spite of this, both

Riflemen escaped injury.

Eventually the Spanish General sent an aide-de-camp with a flag of truce to summon Colonel Craufurd to surrender. Plunkett seeing this easy target said to Fisher, "I'll have a slap at the fellow with the white handkerchief." He then fired two shots at the Spanish flag carrier, sending a rifle-ball through each of his thighs. Three days later this officer died from his wounds. The Spanish were rightly up in arms over this piece of treachery, calling the British a barbarous people. Though this was a mark against Tom's character it was believed, at the time, to be justified, and that the Spanish General was really only playing for time being no more than a ploy to get in rear of the column without any further loss. Craufurd's detachment continued to hold out a little longer but once the ammunition began to run out the game was up and he was forced to surrender. Luckily for Plunkett he was never taken to task by the Spanish, though it would have been hard to single him out from the ranks of his comrades without inside information. Years later (this had to be before 1843) Captain Miller met Plunkett in London and asked him how many men he had shot dead that day. "I think I killed about twenty, sir; I shot a gentleman with a flag of truce, sir" was his reply. On returning to England Plunkett is shown as being in the regimental hospital in the March of 1808, whether the late campaign was the cause is not clear but it could have been brought on by the long sea journey for the troops had spent around nine months onboard ship.
The losses amongst the 95th were:

1st Battalion - 5 companies.
Captain Jenkinson, 2 sergeants, 2 buglers and 36 rank and file killed, Lieutenant Turner died of wounds; Captain O'Hare,

Lieutenant's Cadoux and Macleod severely wounded; Major's Macleod and Travers and Lieutenant McCullouch wounded slightly, 8 sergeants, 2 buglers and 73 rank and file were missing.

2nd Battalion - 3 companies.
3 sergeants, 1 bugler and 46 rank and file killed, Lieutenants Milland and Scott, 6 sergeants and 40 rank and file wounded.

The total losses in killed and wounded in the 8 Rifle companies were: 10 officers and 219 other ranks out of an effective strength of 24 officers and 580 other ranks!

In June 1808 Thomas Plunkett is recorded in the musters as having transferred into Captain Ramadge's company, then shortly afterwards back to his previous company. On the 18th September he embarked for the Continent, now in Captain George Miller's number eight company along with three other 1st Battalion companies. They were part of General Baird's force that landed in Northern Spain having been hastily assembled to join up with Sir John Moore, only to eventually fall back on Corunna.

The early cavalry victories at Benevente and Sahagun were soon over shadowed by the enormity of the task of saving what was possibly the finest British Army ever to leave England's shores from total destruction, leaving Moore with little option but to retreat on Corunna. It was during the retreat and the action at Cacabelos that Plunkett made his claim to fame. Just how this came about is worth expanding on here, the British divisions were moving into the mountains at this time with the rearguard struggling in their wake to hold the French at bay. The weather had changed once more, due to the wind dropping, the snow having turned to sleet and then rain, which made the mountain tracks slippery seas of mud. The 1st Battalion Rifles, having taken over rearguard duty from the 2nd Battalion, upon reaching the town of Bembibre were astonished at the sight that greeted them. It had been a pretty abysmal place prior to this but now it was a thousand times worse for it had been systematically destroyed by the divisions of Baird, Hope and Fraser. The town's main function had been for the storage of wine brought in from the surrounding area, which was kept in underground vats. Every dwelling had been completely vandalized in search of food and the wine. Many of the perpetrators of this wanton destruction were still occupying the village, lying about the streets amongst the debris in a drunken stupor, including many women and children! A number of the women were receiving special attention from the soldiers and muleteers, being in no condition to resist them, even if they wanted to. Captain Miller states that the retreating army left four hundred men completely intoxicated, with a further ten or twelve hundred as stragglers at the village of Bembibre; the rearguard tried their best to animate these sorry souls at the point of the bayonet into leaving the town. Eventually the French arrived at the outskirts of the town, their advanced guard forcing the Riflemen and the 15th Hussars to abandon the place and whoever was left behind to their fate. The French cavalry charged into the streets and immediately started slashing left and right at anything that moved, then took their frustration out on the numerous prostrate bodies, showing no mercy, except to some of women whom they spared only long enough to use for their own amusement and pleasure. Once their lust was satisfied they put them to the sword. Paget's rearguard headed for Cacabelos, leaving a company of the 95th with the Hussars at the village of Cabilos, with two more in advance as out-lying piquets. Sir John Moore in an attempt to prevent the complete disintegration of his army was also making for Cacabelos with his staff. Paget was conducting a punishment parade at the time, due to a large number of his men defying his orders during the night of the 2nd January. The following morning those caught were being flogged systematically, one after the other, while a couple were waiting to be executed for more serious crimes. It was Moore's intention to appeal to the division's former good discipline and sense of duty. Without it, his army would be lost. At Villafranca the divisions had broken out in open rebellion, rioting and breaking into all the dwellings, plundering everything they could lay their hands on. The British commissariat had stock piled numerous stores of food, clothing, ammunition, and medical supplies in the town, which all suffered the same fate. On the 3rd January 1809 the French were approaching within four to five miles of Cacabelos when on reaching some high ground found to their surprise that only a small force was opposed to them. Moore, however, was convinced his rearguard was both strong and good enough to hold the French back and gain him enough time to get his divisions to quit Villafranca and continue on to Lugo and Corunna.

The village of Cacabelos was situated in a valley on the main road some six miles east of Villafranca; here a tributary of the river Sil, the Cua, wound its way close to the village. Though not a wide obstacle it was quite deep at this time of the year. At Cacabelos it was crossed by a small stone bridge flanked by a number of vineyards that were enclosed by hedges and walls that ran parallel to the river. The ground rose gradually from the bridge on the Villafranca side to a height of about 500 yards, giving a commanding view of Cacabelos and the surrounding area. It was from this advantage point that Moore and Paget conducted the defence of the village, being ideally situated to observe any possible attempt to outflank it.

Action At Cacabelos
3ʳᵈ January 1809
*The high ground between **A** and **B** masked the British position from the French cavalry division who, as a result, made a more cautious advance on the British. Paget's punishment parade took place at **A** under cover of the hills at **C**. Once the French reached **E** they were able to see how small the force was opposed to them, for the main body of the 1ˢᵗ Bn 95ᵗʰ Rifles had by this time retired to **D**. The regiments of the Reserve eventually crossed the bridge to take up their positions on the ground beyond the church, leaving only the two remaining Rifle companies and hussars to fall back through the village, with the 28ᵗʰ Light company formed up at the bridge. The Rifle companies formed across the road close to **A**, from which it is easy to see how the French were able to get in rear of them via the road from Cabilos. GC/RC.*

Colonel Beckwith left his two senior Rifle Companies, those of Captain Stewart and O'Hare under Major Norcott to act as his own rearguard out in advance of the company positioned at Cabilos, (which was probably Captain Elder's). He ordered the remaining companies to start falling back towards the village. Paget's punishment parade was still in progress when the first Riflemen arrived with the whole division still on the enemy side of the bridge. It was only at this point when the French opened up on the advanced Rifle Companies that the situation was felt serious enough to abandon the punishment parade but then only

19

after Paget received assurance from the men to continue the previous good conduct of the division. The 52nd were ordered at once to cross the bridge and line the opposite bank to cover the rest of the division and the guns of the Royal Horse Artillery. Moore and Paget still remained on the enemy side of the bridge at this point, watching the gradual withdrawal of the 20th, 28th and 91st Regiments across the bridge, leaving only the Light Company of the 28th on the enemy side to cover the final withdrawal of the Rifles and Hussars. The French cavalry were making ground on the retreating Rifle advanced companies, while one wing had already reached the bridge and was starting to cross to join the rest of the division. Suddenly the first of the rearguard Riflemen came charging into the streets nearest the entrance of the bridge and were soon followed by a number of the leading French cavalry. Moore and his staff were caught up in the chaos of the situation and only just managed to get across the bridge to safety along with Paget. Major Norcott, seeing that a number of his men had already been over taken by the French cavalry, who were hacking at them as they tried to dodge the lethal blows, immediately drew those closest to him across the road and ordered a volley to be fired into the advancing horsemen. The 28th Light Company and the Rifles were now all mixed up trying to gain the safety of the Cacabelos side of the bridge. Norcott ordered the remaining Riflemen to take shelter in the nearest buildings, from where they would be able to defend themselves, while at the same time inflicting further casualties on the French. Those still out in the open were being mercilessly chopped and slashed at by the French cavalry until the 15th Hussars came to their rescue and now a most ferocious hand-to-hand combat took place. One Chasseur was decapitated by a single blow from a Hussar blade. The Riflemen immediately ceased the chance to escape the protection of the houses, made for the bridge where they joined their reserve wing under the command of Colonel Beckwith, lining the walls of the opposite bank. Though a number did fall into the hands of the French who, having reached the area around the bridge in large numbers were able to cut them off, most of those captured belonged to Captain Stewart's company. The French had brought up a number of their own light troops by this time on the back of the horses of their own cavalry to help counter the fire from the Riflemen; all were soon in a fierce fire fight across the short expanse of the river that separated them. It appears to be only at this point Plunkett became involved in the action.

Tom Plunkett was being transported at this time sick in a hospital wagon to the rear, which must have already crossed the bridge spanning the river. On hearing that his company was about to go into action he quickly retrieved his rifle, and without the doctor's knowledge slipped out of the rear of the wagon. He then joined his company, posting himself close to the main road, by this time the enemy were advancing steadily towards the Rifles' position. A shrapnel shell burst in the middle of the advancing French cavalry blowing a large gap completely through the centre of the column bringing them to an immediate halt. They seemed to be quite shaken by this event according to Miller. From the British lines it then looked as if volunteers were called for, as a number of French horsemen advanced independently from different parts of their cavalry formation, until about forty had gathered around two senior officers. They then galloped forward headed by Generals Colbert and Goulieu in an attempt to capture the guns that had done such damage amongst their comrades. The British gunners were too clever for them, quickly limbered up and retired. The party of French horse were not going to be deprived of their prize and charged after the retreating artillery. To capture the guns however, the French horsemen would have to run the gauntlet of a severe rifle fire and cross the bridge, for Captain Miller's company with Plunkett now returned to its ranks, flanked one side of the main road, while two further Rifle companies were positioned on the other side opposite to them. The Riflemen immediately poured a destructive fire into the French cavalry and succeeded in emptying a number of saddles. It is at this point that Captain Miller says Plunkett shot General Colbert! It was General Goulieu however that he noted as being most conspicuous mounted on a white horse! This encouraged Colonel Thomas Graham[4] (who Miller calls Lord Lynedoch a title he attained at a later date) one of Sir John Moore's staff to shout out, "I'll give two guineas to any man who shoots the fellow on the white horse!' Plunkett stepped forward saying, "Please your honour, it won't cost you a tester,' then sent a number of shots after the French General, missing him every time, as did a number of other Riflemen who were eager to avail themselves of the two guineas. Credit has to be given to General Goulieu for he rode bravely through this lottery of rifle-balls escaping unharmed. A number of loose horses were now milling about the road making a great prize for those who could claim them. Lieutenant Jonathan Layton of the Rifles thought this was an opportunity not to be missed. He jumped onto the back of one of the nearest mounts but had only ridden a short distance when in the smoke and confusion of the action, Plunkett spying the imperial eagle on the saddle-cloth thinking it to be a Frenchman, fired at the rider. Fortunately for

---

[4] Colonel Thomas Graham had a severe hatred of revolutionary France; which stemmed from the time his beautiful wife died of consumption in the Mediterranean. Her coffin, on its return to England via Toulouse, had been broken open by drunken soldiers who thought it contained arms for their enemies.

Layton he missed, but shot the horse dead. Lieutenant Layton was most indignant at losing his prize, commented to Captain Miller, "He shot my horse". Miller told him to think himself particularly fortunate that he was not shot himself for he had been the intended target! During the action Miller observed that Plunkett had received a shot through the sleeve of his coat which slightly wounded his wrist but undaunted he continued at his post.

Miller states Plunkett was made Sergeant for his gallant conduct on this occasion. It is quite clear from the muster rolls however, that he remained a private and was in this rank when landing back in England. The Rifles after this action remained at the bridge continuing to provide the rear guard until about ten o' clock that same night when they were ordered to follow their rear guard, but told to proceed with as much stealth as possible, so as not to alert the enemy of their retreat, wagon wheels were wrapped in rags and padded out with moss, grass or any other such component. The next incident though not involving Plunkett is interesting, especially in view of what had happened to Colbert and Goulieu earlier. Unfortunately when researching my book "Rifle Green in the Peninsula" volume one, which also covers the Corunna Campaign, Miller's notes had not been brought to my attention. The reader however will still find a most in-depth account for this action, along with graphic detail of the plight of the Riflemen and their wives during this most harrowing retreat.

The Rifles and rearguard continued to be pressed by the French advance guard but now with a vengeance, led by Goulieu. No doubt they were full of anger at the manner in which Colbert had met his death. The day after leaving Cacabelos Captain Miller's company, now the most rear company of the rearguard, along with some dragoons, came upon some confusion on the road ahead. A number of carts were stopped in the middle of the road for the poor bullocks pulling them had reached the point of no return, they were completely exhausted. It was what the carts were carrying however, that was the cause of so much commotion, for they were full of bags of silver dollars, part of the Military chest! Both officers and men were helping themselves to this money, which at any moment would fall into the hands of the French. Only a small amount was eventually taken by the British, for Goulieu charged them with his cavalry. Miller's Riflemen had no time to contemplate helping themselves to this windfall; their first thought was one of self preservation. They were running for their lives along a road with a steep bank on one side and on the other a deep ravine. Finally they reached a bend in the road. Here the Riflemen scrambled for cover gasping for breath behind some stone walls. This at least allowed them sufficient protection to meet the advancing French and regain their breath.

General Goulieu meanwhile had halted his column to let the men plunder the carts of their silver, while he continued a little further along the road to water his horse. Unbeknown to the general this brought him to within a hundred yards of the concealed Riflemen. With such a prize and opportunity presenting itself, Captain Miller and his officers seized the chance of gaining instant glory; those with rifles were determined to bring down their tormentor. Millers' rifle flashed in the pan and while clearing the touch hole, a Rifleman by the name of Matthews standing next to him shot the French General through the body and the gallant Goulieu fell dead from his horse. There were two Riflemen named Matthews in Miller's company at this time, Michael and Samuel.

It was while researching the Corunna section for volume one on the Rifles that I came across a passage similar to the above where, to prevent the carts containing money from falling into enemy hands, the British cavalry were ordered to carry as much as they could upon their horses in sacks. The rest was then rolled down the ravines in barrels. If the money was in barrels then the cavalry would not have found it so easy to carry away. However, if it was in bags, as Miller states, then at least it would have been feasible. The incident described by Captain Miller of course could have had nothing to do with what I had previously read; if not, there is the possibility they were part of the same convoy[5].

The history of the 28th Regiment however, by Charles Cadell expands on this subject:

> On the morning of the 5th, the reserve left Nogales. We were detained at a bridge a little way on the road, covering the engineers, who were endeavouring to destroy it, but they did not succeed. The 28th Regiment

---

[5] The wife of a sergeant in the 52nd had amassed a large amount of silver coins about her person to carry back to England, it was reported that when boarding one of the Transports at Corunna, she fell into the sea and the weight of the coins sent her straight to the bottom of the harbour and she drowned. It could have been at this part in the retreat that she gained her wealth!

was now the rear-guard of the reserve; and the flank companies, with a company of the '95th Rifles,' formed the rear-guard of the regiment. The whole distance was a continued skirmish. About noon we came up with two cars (sic) laden with dollars; but the bullocks that drew them being completely exhausted, it was impossible to save the treasure. Under these circumstances, Sir John Moore decided that the whole should be thrown down the mountain, most judiciously considering that if the casks were broken, the men would have made a rush for the money, which would have caused great confusion, and might have cost the lives of many. The rear-guard, therefore, were halted; Lieutenant Bennet of the light company, 28th regiment, was placed over the money, with strict orders from Sir John Moore to shoot the first person who attempted to touch it. It was then rolled over the precipice; the casks were soon broken by the rugged rocks, and the dollars falling out, rolled over the height, a sparkling cascade of silver. The French advanced guard coming up shortly after to the spot were detained for a time picking up the few dollars that had been scattered on the road.

The similarity with Miller's account is too close to the 28th Regiment's for them not to be describing the same scenario. Cadell corroborates Miller's version that one company of the 95th were also with them.

It is interesting to note that it was another Rifleman who shot (General) Goulieu and not Plunkett, of whom there is no mention. Yet it is the shooting of Colbert that has been immortalised in the Regiment's history, while Matthews and the unfortunate Goulieu have been air-brushed out of history!

There could be a simpler reason for this omission. I have so far been unable to establish who the unfortunate General Goulieu was, let alone the manner of his death! It is questionable but not impossible that two senior officers would take part in such a dangerous undertaking, though over confidence could have been a factor. There is no record of Goulieu in George Six's *Dictonaire Biographique des Generaux & Amiraux Français de la Revolution et de l'Empire* Paris 1934 which purported to be *the* authoritative French work on the subject. It is interesting therefore to know how Miller could be so specific on the name of an officer who was obviously not a general or possibly even a Colonel. Goulieu might have been no more than a junior officer or Aide to Colbert with the French advanced guard and his death not thought as dramatic to the French, hence there being no record of it? If this is the case, how did Miller come by such information and be so sure of his name? Was this obtained by the plundering of his body, maybe the name found on him in some form of document? There is the chance of course what ever written evidence found was not that belonging to the fallen officer. This is all pure speculation on my part! Unfortunately we will probably never know the truth, unless some hitherto source or document comes to light to explain who the fallen officer was or confirms Goulieu. Whatever written evidence might have been found on Goulieu's body it would have been in French, so we can be certain the name of Goulieu was not provided verbally by the Riflemen. The shooting of Colbert as described in Costello's book tells of Colbert's trumpeter being also killed while the French version has Colbert seeing his aide-de-camp, Lieutenant de la Tour Maubourg shot first! Could the death of Goulieu and Colbert be the two incidents which have some how merged into one? Was Goulieu really the aide?

The death of Goulieu or whoever was commanding the French troops, at least gave the Riflemen some respite from the pressing French cavalry whose ardour had been dampened with the death of another of their generals. The lack of interest in continuing the pursuit of the Riflemen could of course be down to the actions of the French advanced guard in trying to recover as much of the discarded coins as time would allow. Throughout the Peninsula War the French ability to systematic plundering is legendary. The action of the lone Goulieu therefore could just be a case of the French advanced guard not following their officer so they could plunder the carts. The Riflemen now continued pressing on after Moore's retreating army as far as Lugo. Miller states that Plunkett was often found missing from the company during this time only for a shot to ring out when he would reappear with some provisions, these he would share with his Captain. During these days of starvation Miller never asked how he obtained these items, for he was just grateful for their sustenance. The last time Miller mentions Plunkett on the actual retreat is when he and a sergeant concealed themselves in a copse close to the road where the French would eventually pass. The two Riflemen waited patiently for their prey to put in an appearance. Four French horsemen, part of the enemy advanced guard, finally obliged by halting at a point just in front of where they were hidden. Taking deliberate aim each brought his man to the ground. This small token of resistance by the rear guard however was enough to halt the French pursuit for the day! The General, (Miller doesn't say who but I would assume it was Paget, as he was in command of the rear guard) rode up to the two Riflemen and gave them what money he possessed in his pocket. Here we have mention of another monetary reward which is similar to the shooting of Colbert.

The final mention of Plunkett in this campaign comes at the Battle of Corunna. Miller brings an interesting observation to our notice here. During the battle on the heights of Elvina the Rifles ran out of ammunition! This was when they were in a most advantageous position advancing against the French, who were wavering from the severe flanking fire they were receiving, until it gradually dwindled away. The French then had the upper hand. With the situation completely reversed the Riflemen were driven from the heights. On reaching the foot of the hill Captain Miller looking for a quick avenue of escape, found he had run into a garden that was in fact a complete cul-de-sac and trapped by its high walls. With great difficulty he eventually managed to climb one of these. On reaching the top he was just about to jump to safety when a shout came from below. Plunkett had followed him into the garden and was in the same predicament he had been in, the difference however was he could not climb the wall. Miller turned and reaching down told Plunkett to hold his rifle up towards him; grabbing hold of the muzzle he pulled his comrade to safety. On the opposite side the 52nd Regiment were advancing to their support and drove the French back. Had Miller not saved Plunkett there is no doubt he would have spent the rest of the war in a French prison. Plunkett's kindness on the retreat had reaped its reward. Millers' debt had been repaid and they both returned safely to England.

The Plunkett of the pension list discharged in 1817 is without doubt the man generally acknowledged in the regimental history, written and compiled by Sir William Cope. Miller's is the only source material I have found to confirm Plunkett's service in South America. Therefore, it is safe to say Cope derived this information from Miller's account. The same source also provides the name of Fisher at Buenos Aires another expert with the rifle, again mentioned by Cope. Miller's account was published in the United Services Journal, June 1842 to September 1843 but they were un-signed. Cope never made the connection with Miller, therefore was unable to attribute this account to a specific Rifles officer. As far as I am aware no other historian has proven Captain George Miller of the 95th Rifles was the writer of these notes. This prime source material has hardly been accessed, the only written evidence in establishing Plunkett's expertise with the rifle. What is equally important, it was written by a Rifleman who witnessed all the relevant events first hand. Colonel Verner, who took up the mantle of regimental historian after the death of Sir William, adds nothing new to the debate. His own in-depth version of the Regimental History covering the years 1800-1813, keeps to the Costello version of the shooting of Colbert, which suggests, if he had sight of the Miller articles then he never questioned them. I can only think that this was because like Cope, he could not be sure who the writer of the articles was. Cope's history was not published until 1877, over thirty years after Captain Miller's death.

During my research into Plunkett I did come across the name of a John Fisher being awarded a regimental medal for the storming of Badajoz. Whether he is the same Fisher who served with Plunkett in South America I have not been able to confirm. Interestingly Edward Costello's first factual account of Plunkett comes when he witnesses him being awarded a regimental medal, after returning to England from the Corunna Campaign. It is only from this point however that we can take whatever Costello tells us of Plunkett as having any factual content. Anything he writes of Plunkett prior to 1809 is based purely on hearsay. No doubt much of this expanded in the telling, growing eventually out of all proportion to the actual deed, namely the shooting of General Colbert!

The fact that Plunkett shot an unarmed man holding a flag of truce would be met with alarm in these modern times. No fault could really be attached to Plunkett on this occasion; he had been given the task of shooting down as many of the enemy as it was physically possible. Plunkett was obviously ignorant of the conventions of war that surrounded such proceedings. Though it would have shocked his officers, they would have made allowances for the circumstances in which it occurred. There is no evidence that Plunkett was taken to task over this unfortunate incident, and rightly so. He certainly never lost any standing in Captain George Miller's estimation. Plunkett and Fisher's actions, though important at the time, were hardly likely to have warranted any external sign of appreciation such as a medal, under the circumstances, but if the Badajoz Fisher is the same man then they both were eventually honoured. The issuing of these medals should not be taken lightly. The criteria for their issue were quite specific:

"Distinguished marks of courage and voluntary acts of generosity towards either an enemy, or those who are in an enemy's country, it is the intention that two medals of honour shall be instated as reward, a brass[6] medal and a silver one; the ad judgment of either of these medals must be by a board of five Officers of the Corps, in the presence of the same number of Sergeants, Corporals, and private Riflemen, who are to give their votes for the soldier of merit receiving the medal, by the unanimity of

---

[6] I have not seen a brass regimental medal awarded to the 95th in my research into the medals of the Regiment.

voices present, the juniors or private men voting first, after any such act of valour, or generosity in the field, as may appear to the commanding officer worthy of being laid before such board"

Returning to Plunkett's shooting of General Colbert. Miller's account is interesting for what it does not say, which requires examination along with the points he does make. The Regimental Surgeon would have confirmed whether Plunkett was in a fit enough condition to serve with his company. The fact that he was being transported in a hospital wagon suggests he was not. Normal procedure when a man was officially found to be sick or wounded was to have his weapon and knapsack taken from him, then issue him with a chit which vouched for his absence from duty.

Facsimile of an 1816 sickness chit

These were not normal circumstances so a chit was probably not issued. Miller being Plunkett's company commander would have had first hand knowledge as to the reason for his absence, especially as they had some special kind of bond. His platoon sergeant would have brought his absence to his notice if he had not already been aware of the situation. Plunkett, on hearing that his company was about to go into action, slipped away from the hospital wagon without the doctor's knowledge after collecting his rifle. This raises the question, just how sick was he? If what Edward Costello tells us of his short comings are true, which seem highly likely, we have to question was Plunkett as ill as he was making out? His bravery is not an issue here for as we will see later he certainly seems to have enjoyed pitting his skill against the French. What happened next suggests that whatever the truth, the sickness was not that debilitating to have prevented him from taking part in the action! Suddenly he was capable of joining the rest of his company, continuing the retreat without falling out, and taking part in countless skirmishes, then the final Battle of Corunna, has all the signs of a man who was feigning illness! One has to ask, did Plunkett use the special relationship he seems to have formed with Captain Miller to his own advantage? How was he able to convince the Regimental Surgeon he was so ill that he required transportation? There is obviously more to this than we will ever know. My own suspicion, based on the research I have completed, points me into making the assumption that Plunkett's condition was more than likely to be drink related, an ever present factor that continued to blight his character. It is also a known fact that at Cacabelos some of Paget's division devised ways of helping themselves to the wine that was still on offer even though it was heavily guarded. It is hard therefore to believe that Plunkett could have resisted such a temptation. If this was the case and he was no more than the worse for wear due to drink, did Miller have Plunkett taken off as sick rather than see his comrade punished by Paget?

Miller makes no specific mention as to when Plunkett shot General Colbert, or of exacting the same fate to his trumpeter.[7] He mentions only in passing Plunkett's shooting of Colbert, yet gives a detailed account of the failed attempt to shoot General Goulieu. Reading his description of the action along with the hearsay version recorded by Costello it is easy to see the similarities. Miller's is the only factual recorded account, therefore has to be regarded as the sole source from which all details of the incident are based. Having said that, Costello was already in-print by the time Miller sent his recollections to the editor of the United Services Journal. Therefore was it written as a direct result of reading the book or already having seen the earlier version in the US journal in 1839, with which he was not happy! Maybe, not wanting to discredit Costello - a fellow Rifleman - in open debate, this was the easier option? Miller confirms Plunkett joined his company when it had been posted along the side of the main road, but makes no mention of him leaving his position to a point in advance of the company to take an aimed shot at the advancing Colbert, let alone throwing himself down on his back with his foot in the rifle sling to make a deliberate and steadier shot. By this time it is clear that Colbert's cavalry were in the vicinity of the bridge and if they crossed it to attack the guns this has to be around the more likely period when he was shot.

The fact that Plunkett failed to hit Goulieu or Lieutenant Layton who was at a much closer range than the supposed distant shot taken at Colbert is quite intriguing, though we have to take into account that both these individuals would have been highly animated targets at the time, making a snap shot all the harder.

---

[7] See Rifle Green in the Peninsula volume one, p131 for a full account of this action.

General Goulieu's death at the hands of Rifleman Matthews is passed over completely by Cope and Verner in our regimental history, which is most mysterious considering they were both willing to use other parts of Miller's account. For Verner to have changed Cope's version of the shooting of Colbert in his own history, tells me he was reluctant to raise doubt over a piece of famous Regimental lore! Miller's statement that Plunkett received a slight wound through the sleeve of his coat suggests he was wearing his 'greatcoat' which one would expect in such cold conditions. This item of clothing however could only hinder a man who was supposed to be sick, in running out from the security of his position, lying down on his back to take what has been described or passed down through the years as an extremely difficult distance shot. Some much exaggerated claims have been made on the internet to the distance involved in the shooting of Colbert some stating a range of up to 800 yards!

It is clear from what Miller has told us, Plunkett was a cool, calculated Rifleman when it came to his skill at arms, first in South America and later with a Rifle Sergeant near Lugo, taking advantage of the cover available so as not to be exposed to danger. Therefore, one has to ask why would a sickly Plunkett advance to an exposed position, lay on his back to shoot at a target that in a matter of minutes was about to ride past his more secure position, let alone load and take aim and produce another shot of unknown distance that supposedly killed his trumpeter? Taken collectively there seems to be no logic to the supposed shooting of Colbert as laid down in our history. Because Miller gave no detailed description of the shooting of Colbert, this suggests there was nothing remarkable about the incident. Had he not mentioned Plunkett as having shot Colbert then the scenario concerning Goulieu would have been much more significant. There seems to be no problem concerning the actual shooting of Colbert by Plunkett other than the manner in which it was executed. What was remarkable to Miller was the fact he missed Goulieu and later the fortunate Layton! If Captain Miller had suddenly seen Plunkett, who he believed was on his way to hospital, go running out in advance of his position in full view of his company he would have told us. After all, the minor incident with Layton is given the full treatment, though it was not so minor to the Lieutenant. Referring back to Layton's great escape we can safely say this was his second known piece of luck, for in 1808 when going on active service with the regiment he was confronted on the road outside Harwich by the 22 year old Captain Brodie Grant of the Rifles. These two officers are believed to have had a disagreement the night before over the fact that Lieutenant Layton was proceeding on active service while the Captain was obliged to remain in England. This meeting on the road ended with the two Rifles' officers making for the coast, where on the beach concealed by the surrounding heights, accompanied by their seconds they fought a duel with pistols. The result being, after two shots were fired, Grant received a bullet through the spine which killed him. The incident being brought to the notice of the local authorities meant Lieutenant Layton was prevented from going on active service and had to go before the courts. He was acquitted of any wrong doing over Grant's death and the incident was glossed over in the regiment, though not forgotten. Layton never went any further in rank than Lieutenant. He was wounded twice at Waterloo still in the rank of Lieutenant, while officers less senior gained higher rank. From what Miller has written about the action at Cacabelos it would appear his company was in the wing of Riflemen who were first to cross the bridge. Miller's company are shown as having two men missing and no casualties in the returns.

Therefore, if Plunkett advanced from Miller's position to take a closer shot at Colbert this would have meant crossing the bridge.

I have extracted the following known casualties and missing for the 3rd January 1809:

Officers:
Captain Latham Bennett wounded, died of his wounds on the 11th January 1809.
Lieutenant Charles Eeles wounded.

No 1 Company Captain Stewart:
Died:
Riflemen Thomas Phillips, Joseph Rhodes and John Stott.
Missing:
Sergeant Ishmael Cooke (POW), Corporals George Crookshanks, John Winterbottom, Riflemen Joseph Adkins, Henry Barbrook, Charles Cassody, Zacharia Dent, Robert Ewen, William Harry, John Johnson, Archibald Lacky, James Lee, Witherington Lee, Donald McIntire, Joseph Moore, Hugh Paisley[8] (POW), Peter Phoss, Richard Rice, John Richards, James Ridley, James Ross, Joseph Sipson, Daniel Smith, Patrick Stanton, John Sturges, George Sweeney, Charles Turner, Benjamin Tuttle. (31)

No 2 company Captain Ross:
Died:
Riflemen James Darrett, John McDonough.

---

[8] Hugh Paisley was awarded the Naval General Service medal in 1848 with the clasp Copenhagen, and spent the whole of the war as a prisoner, therefore not entitled to the Military General Service medal 1848.

Missing:
Corporal James McKenzie, Bugler John Harvey, Riflemen Robert Boyd, Robert Briggs, Andrew Clarke, John Cope, Laurence Dooly, Richard Fanning, Thomas Hill, George Pitt, William Swan, and William Thornton. (14)

No 3 Company Captain O'Hare:
Died:
Rifleman William Cleaver, KIA.
Missing:
Riflemen Isaac Fiddler, Lawrence Kinchlow, William Livermore, and John Piper. (5)

No 4 Company Captain Beckwith:
Missing:
Bugler Patrick Mitchell, Riflemen Joseph Betson, Edward Williams, Brooks Wright. (4)

No 5 Company Captain Pakenham/Bennett (?):
(Lieutenant Layton was in this company)

No 6 Company Captain Ramadge:
Died:
Sergeant Mathew Alison KIA.
Missing:
Buglers Brien McGrath, Brien Tierney, Riflemen George Tomkins, and William Townsend. (5)

No 7 Company Captain Cameron:
Died:
Rifleman Adam Ross KIA. (1)

No 8 Company Captain Miller:

Missing:
Riflemen Joseph Billings, James Curran. (2)

No 9 Company Captain Elder:
Died:
Riflemen William Burroughs, Lauchiston Curry, James Esky KIA, William Reynolds KIA, and Richard Woods KIA.
Missing:
Riflemen William Edmonds, Edward Evans, and Jonathan Underton. (8)

It is easy to see how previous chroniclers of our regimental history have repeated the inaccuracies surrounding the shooting of Colbert by Plunkett, as I had done until undertaking this in-depth look at the facts surrounding the account. Edward Costello's memoirs however do give us a unique insight into Plunkett's character from the ordinary Rifleman's point of view. Many historians have used his account as background when researching the Rifles for the Peninsula and Waterloo periods. This does not mean however that he should never be questioned; otherwise we are all guilty for the constant repetition of these errors in our publications. It is not always acceptable to have regimental history questioned, or changed, but it should never be set in stone. For many, even to this day, Sir William Cope is regarded as the last word with his *History of the Rifle Brigade.* An example of how I was personally questioned for daring to upstage such a well known historian as Sir Arthur Bryant, who wrote the book, *Jackets of Green*, though a lesser known authority on Rifle history than Cope, came about when I once asked permission from a lady to use some of her original letters dealing with the Crimea, written by a private Rifleman. This was while researching my book *Rifle Green in the Crimea*, to which she replied, "what more could I add to Bryant's writings on the campaign?" He had published his book in 1972 as a general history of the Rifle Brigade. Bryant covered the Crimea reasonably well within the limits of a general history but could not be expected to accomplish what was researched for a whole book! It is quite easy therefore, to see why Cope was considered unquestionable - that is until Colonel Verner started writing his version of the regimental history in which he found errors in Cope's work. Verner however, did not start producing his history until after Cope's death. Most rigorous in his quest for accuracy, Colonel Willoughby Verner was not the sort of man to suffer fools gladly, but he still repeated some of Cope's errors. I have tried to eliminate as many of these as possible in my own works, not forgetting I have in some instances had access to documents and research not available to these two brilliant regimental historians. It is interesting however, that while the regiment was willing to accept the findings of Verner and not question these alterations, they are reluctant to accept modern research highlighting the history which is much more in-depth and accurate.

The Sharpe series produced on the back of the popular novels written by Bernard Cornwell are great publicity for the regiment, and while most grateful to Mr. Cornwell and the power of television for bringing the "Rifles" into the homes of so many ordinary people, it did come with some unwanted baggage. A myth has since started to build up around the 95th Rifles, with some individuals even going as far as to proclaim they were the SAS of their day! This is absurd, some re-enactors have even taken this on board, and if left unchallenged it is only a matter of time before fiction is quoted as fact. Some re-enactors I have seen have become mixed in their portrayal of the 95th, whereas it would be better if they stuck to the period if they want to be true living history. One chap I spoke to had the full trappings of a Rifleman with what I can only describe as a 'David Bowie' style knife hanging from his waist belt and a bugle of the later 1860's pattern slung across his shoulder. This chap wanted to be the epitome of everything represented by the Rifles. Buglers did not carry a rifle during this period of history only a sword, longer, but similar in shape and format to the Baker sword bayonet. Others who fancy themselves as officers have taken to wearing reinforced leather pants similar in style to cavalry overalls, in brown tan or black, and hair worn in a cue which was discontinued in 1808. Therefore we can see a mish-mash of styles and equipment being presented to the public to this very day. There are more acceptable changes to the Rifles equipment that would not be questioned, for instance the knife mentioned earlier could have been replaced by a short felling axe of the period, for these were issued so many to a company, and purported to be far superior than the army issued bill-hook. The Light Division using these axes were able to forage and set up a bivouac far quicker than any of the other divisions! Major Norcott set a precedent by having issued to his two 2nd Battalion companies, who were in action at the Battle of Barrosa in March 1811, leather cases to hold the powder flask, which attached to the waist belt, rather than have it slung around the neck - a much more logical solution and something the other companies were in favour of once they saw them. The powder flask I have always maintained was used far more than historians, muzzle loaders and arms experts give credit. My firm belief is that the rifle could not be loaded by using powder from the powder horn, other than by the detachable Irish measure. Norcott expanded on how these items were so often broken and lost. The Riflemen then had to use corks fixed to the end to prevent powder loss or damp penetration. If this was a common case it is easy to see how the powder flask would have become even more indispensable. The cord from which the horn was suspended passed through leather loops attached to the shoulder belt thus restricting its movement, making it most difficult to load the rifle from the short distance from the hip to the weapon. I have always thought the powder horn was more of a main magazine from which the firer replenished the powder flask when empty. This contained enough powder for about thirty shots. It would be far easier to load from this in the most difficult of firing positions, although I am sure paper cartridges were used most of the time. Hollywood has a reputation for distorting British Military history and its achievements to its own ends, which should not be repeated in our own country, but sadly this is also becoming a fact! This book I hope will be the first of many in my personal crusade to eradicate such errors from becoming entrenched in Rifles' history, giving those interested in the Regiment an honest portrayal of a period Rifleman. This applies even more so now that the 'Rifles' have evolved as the largest infantry regiment in the British Army. It would not do for the newly amalgamated regiments to start repeating the deeds of their new regiment, if they are inaccurate. It is interesting to see however that the wheel has turned full circle, the 95th Rifles having gone through a number of name changes over the years, are now back to being called the Rifles!

I will continue with Costello's account of Plunkett, backed up where possible from the records held at (TNA) along with what Captain Miller writes of him during their final years of service.

Captain Miller states that after Corunna, he and Plunkett were a long time parted. We therefore only have Costello's account of what Plunkett got up to until he was invalided to England in 1811.

Costello - also an Irishman - joined the 1/95th Rifles in 1808. He was at Hythe when the battalion returned from Corunna. Here he was able to witness first hand Thomas Plunkett's character when serving in Captain Stewart's No 1 company. Costello was in No 3 company, that of Captain Peter O'Hare the senior captain. By this time Riflemen were already telling the story of Tom's deeds during the recent Corunna Campaign. He describes Tom Plunkett on first setting eyes on the man: 'he was a smart well made fellow, about middle height and in the prime of manhood, with a clear "grey" eye and handsome countenance. He was a general favourite with both officers and men, besides being the best shot in the regiment." It is clear from Costello's description of Plunkett that he is the man in the pension discharge papers. Plunkett would have been about twenty five years of age at this time; 5 feet 6 inches would be classed as middle height at this period of military history. I consulted the records of three hundred Riflemen who fought at Waterloo and the average height worked out at 5 feet 7 inches. Costello also confirms Plunkett's grey eyes.

At this point it would be a good idea to refresh the reader with what Costello actually had to say, or to be more precise what was actually written about the action on the retreat to Corunna in which Thomas Plunkett shot General Colbert. It should be remembered that this is based on verbal accounts given by fellow Riflemen. Many readers' first impression of Corunna will have come from seeing the iconic painting by J.P. Beadle of the 'Rearguard' which has been reproduced numerous times for various publications. The painting depicts Brigadier Robert Craufurd as the focal point of the painting with part of his brigade turning to oppose the enemy as they made for Vigo. The 95th Rifles are shown lining either side of the road on which Craufurd is positioned on his horse. The painting is a master piece of its kind. However, I have yet to hear mention the mistake made by Beadle when painting the Baker rifle, for he shows the brass patch-box on the inside of the rifle butt, the wrong side! My attention was brought to this by James Dann. Craufurd's force was not pursued by the French to Vigo for they were more concerned with the destruction of Sir John Moore's army making for Corunna. Craufurd's task was to ensure he had an alternative embarkation point should this be necessary.

Costello:

"At the retreat to Corunna the Light Brigade was exceedingly hard pressed by the French horse, which was vastly superior. In the neighbourhood of Astorga they made several determined charges, in which a French General named Colbert [Auguste-Marie-Francois Colbert 1777-1809] conspicuous on a grey horse was remarkably active. Although frequently aimed at by our men, he seemed to bear a charmed life, and invariably escaped. In one of the French charges headed by this daring officer, General Sir Edward Paget rode up to the Rifles and offered his purse to any man who would shoot him. Plunkett immediately started from his company. He ran about 100 yards nearer to the enemy, threw himself on his back on the road which was covered in 'snow' placed his foot in the sling of his rifle, and taking deliberate aim, shot General Colbert. Colbert's Trumpet-Major, who rode up to him, shared the same fate from Tom's unerring rifle. Our men, who had been anxiously watching, cheered, and Tom began running in upon the rearmost sections. He was just in time to escape some dozen troopers who chased after him. Our General immediately gave Tom the purse he had promised, with encomiums (high commendation) upon his gallantry. He promised to recommend him to his Colonel, which he did in high terms to Colonel Beckwith. A few days afterwards, when the French attacked Sir John Moore's position at Corunna, Plunkett was again noted for his cool bravery and daring especially in making some admirable shots, by which they lost many officers".

Costello's account first appeared in the United Services Journal No 122 January 1839, which differed slightly from what would eventually be written up in book form, two notable changes being: 'our *general* rode up to the Rifles, and offered any man a purse of gold who would shoot the *obnoxious* Frenchman,' This changed to read: *Paget* instead of general and *daring* in place of obnoxious. So even in the first recorded version of the incident committed to print we have alterations. Why Costello should change the original wording is unclear but it would seem to be the hand of a Mr. Mellor, who it is acknowledged by the editor of the Royal United Services Institute journal as the gentleman who put together Costello's notes and dictation honing the narrative to what we have come to know today. Quarter Master William Surtees does mention the incident in his book *Twenty-five Years in the Rifle Brigade* published in 1833 but only a short paragraph (shown in full later) though he was not present at the time.

It is easy to see how Costello's version has evolved from the factual account given by Captain George Miller, the story changing as it was re-told time after time or added to by the story teller, who no doubt gloried in the event by association. We have all come across this sort of thing I am sure in our own lives. The smoke and confusion of the action cannot be understated, for it caused Plunkett to fire upon one of his own officers; admittedly he was riding a French horse. It is debatable therefore how much the ordinary Rifleman would have witnessed under the same conditions while firing, loading, and trying to preserve their own skin. Sir William Cope in his history raised some doubt as to Paget offering a sum of money to a soldier to slay such a chivalrous and brave enemy, but as we have seen earlier it was Colonel Graham who made such an offer, Miller referring to him as Lord Lyndoch[9] in his article.

---

[9] A title he received later in life

47

What would Miller have gained by inventing such a scenario, telling us in another account how Plunkett and a sergeant of the Rifles were given money for shooting some of the French advanced guard. Cope had reservations about such an act. Miller and his fellow officers certainly had no scruples about shooting a defenceless high ranking officer, no matter how brave he was! Cope, while selective in what he chose to use from Miller's account, was writing history in another era, a period that would have probably frowned upon such activity while at the same time not wishing to upset the Paget family (quite rightly as it turns out when the culprit was Colonel Thomas Graham). The French version of the death of Colbert has him being shot above the left eye knocking him backwards off of his horse which means he was hit from either the front or side, at close range. Therefore he would have been either approaching the bridge, or returning from attacking the guns when he received his fatal blow.

With stirring accounts such as this going around the companies it is with little wonder that the new recruits were in awe of Plunkett's status and all would have liked to emulate his deeds, which can be seen by Costello's description of Plunkett's promotion to corporal.

"The first parade we had after our men received their new equipment is imprinted upon my memory from a particular circumstance calculated to make an impression upon the mind of a youthful soldier, such as I then was. We were formed into hollow square, and ordered to face inwards. We knew it was not a punishment parade, so we naturally expected some address from the commanding officer. We were wondering what was coming, when Colonel Beckwith broke the silence calling

48

out, "Private Thomas Plunkett," as he halted in the finest position of military attention, with his rifle shouldered, within a few paces of his officer. The commanding officer pointed to Plunkett, and then addressing Tom added, "I have ordered a medal for you in approval of your late gallant conduct at Corunna. Present yourself, sir, to the master tailor and get on a corporal's stripes, and I will see you not want for higher promotion, as you continue to deserve it. I love to reward conduct such as yours!" making his salute, Tom retired, and we formed into column and marched back to barracks, desiring the praise that had been bestowed on the fortunate Plunkett."

Costello adds a little postscript to this rosy description of Plunkett:

"However, the truth must be told. Like all heroes, Tom had his faults, and the destructive consequences of one in particular was, in a soldier, calculated to counter balance a thousand virtues, Tom was a thirsty soul, exceedingly fond of a 'drop'. This was his unfortunate failing through life, without which he would have got on in the service."

Costello was right on this count for his discharge papers show Plunkett as being a very bad character and nearly worn out in the service, while the records in the TNA for April-May 1809 pay-list quarter confirm Plunkett was a Corporal in No 1 Company, Captain Stewart's.

What became of Captain George Miller? It would appear he transferred into the 2nd Battalion 95th, severing his immediate link with Plunkett. He had taken part in the Walcheren Expedition in 1809, which became a disaster as hundreds of men died from

49

malaria contacted there, while others suffered for the remainder of their lives. This deprived Wellington of some of his most experienced and greatly needed troops. Miller must have been free from the disease for on the 2nd February 1810 he passed into the senior department at the Royal Military College. Plunkett by then was serving in Portugal having taken part in the famous march under Craufurd on Talavera. Miller's stay at the military college was short lived for on the 7th March 1810 he was ordered to rejoin his regiment for embarkation, but rejoined the military college on the 6th May 1810, only once again to be ordered to join his regiment on 17th June 1810. This time Captain Miller was bound for southern Spain with the 95th Rifles though not in the capacity of a company commander. He was probably part of the Rifles' Staff, and was present at the Battle of Barrosa, 5th March, 1811. He rejoined the military college on the 1st February 1812 and finally passed out on the 20th May 1812, when Miller is noted as being on 'particular service'.

Meanwhile, Thomas Plunkett, according to Costello, had been part of one of the recruiting parties attempting to entice men from the militia to enlist in the Rifles, was entertaining the locals with his special form of dancing and a great attraction. Costello says, the recruiting party with Plunkett had positioned a number of large barrels of beer in strategic parts of the town, with the lids removed, and from which they invited the inhabitants to partake in some of this free refreshment. Once a large crowd had gathered, Plunkett, especially noted for his rendition of the hornpipe, jumped on to the top of one of the un-opened barrels and commenced to entertain the onlookers.

In the middle of his performance, the lid gave way and Plunkett plunged into the barrel and was immersed up to his chin in beer. The crowd fell about in fits of laughter. Plunkett stayed in this position until he had achieved the required effect, suddenly jumped out of the barrel and after giving him a good shake, rushed off to the nearest public house, with the laughing crowd in pursuit. Going inside he disappeared a little way up its open chimney, and then rushed back out into the street shouting to the crowd, "Now I am ready for parade again!" Though extreme in its example Plunkett's action was not lost on the crowd, and

51

served to demonstrate the claim of the Rifles' recruiting posters, that there was no pipe clay and bull in their regiment. Proving their dark uniform needed very little attention. When the 1st Battalion 95th set sail for Portugal under Craufurd along with the 43rd and 52nd Regiments Plunkett continued to entertain the troops on board ship with his dancing. He was a big favourite with the crew of the transport. His rendition of the horn-pipe was an instant hit, in which he added a form of double shuffle in the dance, a movement he had perfected to his advantage.[10]

RIFLE CORPS!

COUNTRYMEN!

LOOK, BEFORE YOU LEAP:

Half the Regiments in the Service are trying to perfuade you to Enlift;

But there is ONE MORE to COME YET!!!

The 95th; or, Rifle REGIMENT,

COMMANDED BY THE HONOURABLE

Major-General Coote Manningham,

The only Regiment of RIFLEMEN in the Service:

THINK, then, and CHOOSE, Whether you will enter into a Battalion Regiment, or prefer being a RIFLEMAN,

The firft of all Services in the Britifh Army.

In this distinguished Service, you will carry a Rifle no heavier than a Fowling-Piece. You will knock down your Enemy at Five Hundred Yards, inftead of missing him at Fifty. Your Clothing is GREEN, and needs no cleaning but a Brush. Those Men who have been in a RIFLE COMPANY, can best tell you the comfort of a GREEN JACKET.

NO WHITE BELTS! NO PIPE CLAY!

On Service, your Post is always the Post of Honour, and your Quarters the best in the Army; for you have the firft of every thing; and at Home you are sure of Respect—because a BRITISH RIFLEMAN always makes himself Respectable.

The RIFLE SERJEANTS are to be found any where, and have orders to Treat their Friends gallantly every where.

If you Enlift, and afterwards wish you had been a RIFLEMAN, do not say you were not asked; for you can BLAME NOBODY BUT YOURSELF.

GOD SAVE the KING! *and his Rifle Regiment!*

HULL, January 11th, 1808.

ROBERT PECK, Printer of the HULL PACKET, Scale-Lane, HULL

---

[10] Probably making him the Michael Flatley of River Dance fame of his day!

However, it is during the winter months of 1809 -1810 that Costello brings to our attention the darker side of Thomas Plunkett:

"Tom had been promoted to the rank of sergeant in the Hon. Captain Stewart's No 1 company. One morning, when the company was on parade Tom appeared quite tipsy. The officers had not yet arrived, and when he gave the words of command for inspection, he set the men laughing. The Pay-Sergeant, his superior in rank, ordered him to desist, but Tom refused. While this altercation was going on Captain Stewart arrived, ordered Tom to be put under arrest and confined to quarters. When sober, Tom was noted for his good humour and humanity, but now left alone, and under the influence of intoxication, he felt that his treatment had been undignified and wanted vengeance. He barricaded the door of the room, and loaded some ten or twelve rifles belonging to men on fatigue duty. Taking up one of these and cocking it, he placed himself at an open window for the purpose, as he stated to several men, that he intended shooting Captain Stewart. Stewart, however, had been forewarned. Meanwhile several of the men at first tried coaxing him out, and then force themselves into the room. Eventually he was induced to relent when Lieutenant William Johnston came up, who was a favourite with the men, Tom opened the door and was made a prisoner. His action could not be passed over lightly and hc was brought before a Regimental Court Martial at which he was found guilty, reduced to the ranks and sentenced to receive 300 lashes.

The sober Plunkett was of course full of remorse. The

men, on hearing of his fate felt sorry for him, this was also the case amongst many of the officers. The pattern for the regiment was now stripped, tied to a tree in the middle of a hollow square for all to witness, his eyes pleading to the officers and men. The bugler whose duty it was to lay on the 'Cat'[11] at first held back from full strokes but he was ordered by Beckwith to, "Do your duty fairly sir!" After the first twenty five lashes another bugler continued the punishment. At the thirty fifth stroke Beckwith ordered a halt and Plunkett was taken down, he then addressed Plunkett, "You see now, sir, how easy it is to commit a black-guards crime, but how difficult it is to take his punishment." Costello continues, "Plunkett appeared to get over the recollection of his former disgrace very quickly, and soon got into favour with his officers again. Even though he still had relapses of little spells of drunkenness he was made corporal, and went through the sanguinary scenes of the Peninsula, unscathed from shot or steel."

Referring back to the documents for Plunkett in the TNA, to confirm Plunkett's promotions and reductions, there is a slight discrepancy. The muster and pay list rolls are pretty accurate when it comes to money. For instance when a man is killed in action his pay is stopped from the moment he is killed. So these very same documents show promotions and payments in a

---

[11] Corporal punishments took place generally on the evening parades. The Bugle-Major had to draw his cat-o'-nine-tails from the Quarter Master Sergeant, for which he had to pay the sum of one shilling, this was charged against the punished Soldier's accounts for that muster. The cat was returned to the Quarter Master Sergeant on completion of the parade. The crime and punishment was then copied into the courts-martial, or black-book of the regiment.

particular rank to the penny. He was reduced to the rank of private on the 15th September 1810. Plunkett's reduction is in keeping with the episode Costello described. However, the following quarter's muster shows him being promoted to Sergeant on the 17th September 1810 only two days after being reduced and flogged! This has to be a clerical error by the clerk or pay-sergeant and probably should read the other way around, in other words promoted on the 15th and reduced on the 17th. This sounds the more logical conclusion and the muster rolls confirm, for he is paid as a private for the remaining time he served in the Peninsula with the 1st Battalion, with no indication of any further promotions to Sergeant or reductions. Costello makes no further references to Plunkett during the Peninsula war for the simple reason; he had been invalided back to England on the 6th December 1811. During this year Plunkett is shown as having a number of spells in hospital. The Battalion are shown as being at Atalaye and Abedon in Spain for the muster quarter 25th June-24th September 1811 and for August and September Plunkett is shown as being in the Divisional Hospital, then in the General Hospital 25th September-5th December and again 11th-15th December, though he was invalided to England on the 6th. In England he is reunited with his friend Captain George Miller who marks the occasion thus:

"When I returned to England (which was probably around the beginning of 1812) I found Plunkett swelled up like a beer barrel and as yellow in the face as a guinea. Upon inquiring the cause of so strange a metamorphosis, I found that a French Dragoon had ridden over him and damaged his internal organs considerably. I thought it was all up with my poor friend; he recovered, however, and serving in a different battalion from me. I gave a sergeant in exchange for him, and away we went, like the Knight of Lamancha, in search of adventures."

It was about this time a detachment had been organised to go out to the Peninsula as reinforcements for the 2nd Battalion. A young Highland officer Sandy Campbell was part of the detachment going with Miller and Plunkett. The first time this young Rifles' officer went into action he was full of admiration at the way Plunkett, his nemesis applied his skill to the rifle. However, his instruction under Plunkett was all too short, for Campbell received a mortal wound in the upper thigh. A handkerchief had been tied around his leg and twisted tight by the use of a ramrod, but he still bled to death. Plunkett having become quite attached to the young officer stayed with him until the end. He then dug a grave with the use of his sword bayonet and buried him close to where he had received his fatal wound. Again it is Plunkett's skill with the rifle that produces comment. Plunkett's skill at arms comes to the fore once more on the heights of Bayonne. Miller:

"...our battalion had some slight skirmishing at long shots. Plunkett and a few men being sent in front, a French officer got up on the top of a bank, apparently in some act of bravado, where he stood a long time, Plunkett firing at him all the while, at a range of about 500 yards. At last, he appeared to us to leap down, but later we saw him carried off in a blanket. A few more Riflemen were then sent down to place themselves on the left of the skirmishers, but they returned shortly after; upon being asked the reason, one of them replied, "Plunkett, sir, says he'll be damned if any man shall go before him." The line then advanced, the skirmishing was sharp. Plunkett was by the side of the road that led towards the enemy, behind a thorn bush; of the two men, who were with him, one

56

was severely wounded and the other killed."

Miller called to Plunkett to come to the cross-road where he was, but he coolly replied, reloading his rifle "must stop here, sir, to keep a look out." The following day after encountering the enemy, their fire slackened, this allowed Plunkett and another Rifleman time to join a group of Portuguese for a bit of fun. Here they noticed two French soldiers carrying a pig across a field; the two Riflemen fired, shooting them both. Then to the amusement of their officers this group provided much entertainment in trying to capture the liberated pig!

The last time we hear of Plunkett in the Peninsula is again from the pen of Captain Miller, this was as he lay in his tent the night of the action previously quoted listening to the men gossiping around the watch fire. It started with the loss of the pig and then of their comrades. "Well", said one "when Tom Turtle was hit, he was well covered as any man could be." "I hardly think so," said another; "for you know he was killed." "well, barrin' a bit of his head, it was as I say". "Plunkett," said another, "I'm as good a soldier as you are." "You a soldier!" was the reply; you're a poor man, sir!" Plunkett then gave them chapter and verse into the art of skirmishing and no tactician did it better. He ended by telling them, "above all things beware of flankin' fire, boys; for if they bring a flankin' fire upon you three men will drive a thousand!"

During the Peninsula War our Riflemen divided the officers into two classes, the 'Come on' and the 'Go on'. Tom Plunkett once observed to an officer, "the words 'go on' don't befit a leader, sir".

The muster rolls do not quite agree with Captain Miller as to

Plunkett's rank. He is shown as having transferred into the 2nd Battalion on the 25th June 1812, with the rank of private, 15th October 1812, in number three company. When he returned with Captain Miller's detachment on the 30th August 1813 he was a Corporal! Miller's company was then numbered No 2. Plunkett remained in this company and with this rank until the 11th May 1815 when he is shown as from corporal to private. There is no mention of him being reduced.

The last word on Plunkett comes from Costello, though at the time he was serving in a different battalion, and on another part of the battle-field. Thomas Plunkett served in Captain George Miller's No 2 company of the 2nd Battalion 95th at Waterloo, 18th June 1815. Edward Costello, wounded at Quatre Bras on the 16th June 1815 had already been taken to Brussels for treatment. There he states he met Plunkett, observing:

"His usual luck forsook him at Waterloo, where a ball struck the peak of his cap and tore his forehead across, leaving a very ugly scar. I had gone wounded to the rear and there saw him under the hands of the surgeon.

Shortly after the battle of Waterloo, Tom wedded a lady remarkable for being deficient in one essential to beauty, i.e. she had no face, or at all events, was so defaced it amounted to the same thing. She had gallantly followed the camp through the war, and this slight flaw in her beauty arose from the bursting of an ammunition-wagon at Quatre Bras, near to which she stood and by which her countenance was rendered a blue shapeless, noseless mass. The event was commemorated by the government allowing the heroin a shilling a day pension. After Waterloo Tom Plunkett was invalided to England, where he passed the board at Chelsea, but disgusted at being awarded 'six' pence a day for his wound and long service, he expressed himself to the Lord Commissioners in a way that induced them to strike him off the list altogether. The following day he started off for Ireland, where he duly arrived in rags and wretchedness. To relieve himself he enlisted again, this time in either the 31st or 32nd Regiments of the line, then Quartered somewhere in the north.

While wearing the red coat, he had a singular meeting with his former colonel, General Sir Sidney Beckwith, which I have often heard him relate. It is customary to have half-yearly inspections of our regiments at home, shortly after Tom enlisted; his regiment was formed for inspection. On one of these occasions, that duty devolved on Sir Sidney, on walking down the front rank, he came to Tom, who was distinguished by two medals on his breast (Waterloo and Regimental) "Do my eyes deceive me?" said Sir Sidney, "surely you are Tom Plunkett, formerly of my own regiment?" "What's left of me, sir," said Tom, who was seldom deficient in a prompt reply. "And what has again brought you in to the service; I thought you had passed the board at Chelsea?" "So I did," said Tom "but they only allowed me sixpence a day, sir, so I told them to keep it for the young soldiers, as it wasn't enough for the old, who had seen all the tough work out". "Ha! The old thing, Tom I perceive," said Sir Sidney. That same day Plunkett was called to be present at the officers' mess where Sir Sidney was being dined. After dinner Tom was sent for and asked to give a toast on being handed a glass of wine. "Then, sir, here's to the immortal memory of the poor fellows who fell in the

Peninsula," said Tom. He was dismissed with a present form Sir Sidney and next day made corporal. Shortly afterward he went before the board at Kilmainham hospital (the Irish equivalent to Chelsea) and was granted one shilling a day."

Costello states:

"Plunkett went to Canada where he was given a parcel of land, along with four years pay for his pension. He did not last the year complaining the land was mainly swamp or forest and the climate bad. He returned to England with his wife; I met Plunkett in Burton Crescent (now called Cartwright Gardens just south of St. Pancras station) in London. He was picturesquely clothed and selling matches. Plunkett stating a man had to do something in those hard times for bread, at the same time passing his hand across the furrow in his brow, made by the bullet at Waterloo! A few months back, while on duty at the tower of London, one of the warders informed me that a most extraordinary lady was anxious to see me. To my astonishment Mrs Plunkett stood before me holding a handkerchief to her face. Between sobs she told me of Tom's death. While passing through Colchester he staggered and fell dead on the spot. His death and the pity for Mrs Plunkett aroused a number of retired officers living in the town to make a collection and £20 was given to the widow, while a lady paid for his burial and raising of a memorial stone,"

So ends the final chapter on Thomas Plunkett, if Costello is to be believed then this would have happened between 1832-3 and 1839. First, I must clear up some points around Costello's meeting at Brussels with the wounded Plunkett. While researching, *Rifle Green at Waterloo* I examined the muster/pay lists for the period of Waterloo and the Quarter immediately after. There is no indication that Plunkett was wounded during this time. The pay-clerk for the 2nd Battalion 95th was the most thorough of all the three battalions in his returns. He marked up the months of each Quarter with 'sick absent' follow by wounded if a casualty at Waterloo, while the 1st Battalion clerk just put 'sick absent' and the 3rd Battalion clerk nothing! If Plunkett had been wounded I am sure it would have been entered in the muster rolls. Would he have married a woman so badly disfigured out of pity just after her accident?

The 2nd Battalion were not at Quatre Bras, therefore Mrs Plunkett would have to have been with another regiment if Plunkett married her after being disfigured. The 1st Battalion was forbidden to take any wives on the Waterloo Campaign by Colonel Barnard. I believe Plunkett was already married or at least involved with this lady prior to Waterloo? An ammunition cart did, however, explode beyond the battlefield on the 19th June 1815 close to the 2nd Battalion position. Could this have been when Mrs Plunkett received her injuries? The pension records confirm Plunkett served for a short time in the 41st Regiment and a Veteran or Militia unit and that he received one shilling per day pension. There is no mention of any wounds which would have been fairly obvious according to Costello's account. I have found no evidence to support Mrs Plunkett receiving a pension and believe this was an unlikely event.

The muster pay lists confirm after Waterloo that when the 2nd Battalion were stationed at the Champs Elysees Plunkett was absent sick during July and August, returning to the battalion in September. They give no indication as to him being wounded which confirms what I have said earlier reference the clerk and the casualty return. His discharge and pension documents make no mention of him being a casualty, leading me to believe he was never a casualty at Waterloo. In November and December 1816 Plunkett is shown as being in the regimental hospital. Then 25 June-23 July 1817, when at Valenciennes, he is invalided to Shorncliffe and discharged 24th July. If Plunkett was really wounded then I have done him a disservice but everything seems to point to him suffering possibly from the injuries caused by the trampling of the dragoons horse in 1811! One would have thought if Plunkett was discharged from the Rifle Brigade he would not have been fit for further service, but on the 13th January 1818 he enlisted into the 41st Regiment who were stationed in Ireland. His service with the Rifle Brigade is noted, confirming we still have the same man. This is further corroboration of Costello's story. He was stationed at Naas and shown on command for February and March, the following muster taken at Londonderry, and again he is at Naas, on duty at Salins in May. In June he is en route for Naas, August in the regimental hospital, and December on duty. The following year he is posted to various locations around the country but in the February 1819 again he is in the regimental hospital. He was discharged from the 41st on the 5th February 1820. Whether it was the soldiering in his blood or the need for employment we will never know but Plunkett appears on the musters of the 2nd Veteran Battalion from October 12, 1820, stating joined from 'Out Pension'. November he was again in hospital, followed by further spells in hospital in February and March when serving in number 6 company. He was discharged on the 24th April 1821, low and behold only to appear on the muster rolls of the 1st Veteran Battalion in December 1821. There is no enlistment date known, for there is a gap in the musters between 25 June-24 December 1821 and he is not shown before these dates. The postings for 1821 to1823 are all around Cork. No further entries show him as being in hospital but the other side of Plunkett seems to have raised its ugly head once more for he is imprisoned, 1st November to the 16th December 1823 when serving in number 9 company. The following year from 25th April to 3rd May, he is again in prison, his final discharge being dated 4th November 1824. The Pension documents have written in the margin the date 1832 and commuted pension which confirms what Costello tells us about him going to Canada.

I had a researcher friend who lives near Colchester check out every angle covering Plunkett's death and possible burial place but with no luck and no sign of a memorial! What further muddies the waters is the Roll of Fame erected in 1929 in Winchester Cathedral on which Riflemen appear only when they are dead, sanctioned by the Rifle Brigade Club. Plunkett's inclusion as with many other entries have been inscribed long after they had died but to give a specific date of 1825 is puzzling. It would be interesting to know how they were able to be so specific in arriving at this precise date. There is nothing in the Rifle Brigade Club files sanctioned by the committee who set up the memorial to indicate a reason for this date. I have found nothing to connect Colchester to the regiment for the period in question. However, in Chichester Cathedral a memorial erected to Lieutenant Edward Madden of the Rifle Brigade who died there in 1826 was donated by his brother officers. Could Costello have confused Colchester with Chichester? I have had no response to a letter I wrote to the local paper in Chichester asking for any known references to Plunkett. Research is still continuing into Plunkett's story, though the signals are mixed as to the manner of his shooting of Colbert, he will always be remembered as the Rifleman with extraordinary ability with the Baker Rifle.

Epilogue

I have used Captain Miller and Edward Costello's accounts along with official documents at (TNA) in my research on Plunkett, though other Riflemen do mention him in their books, for instance Kincaid[12] and Surtees. The latter as stated earlier mentions Plunkett shooting Colbert in his book *Twenty-five years with the Rifle Brigade*:

> The force of the enemy greatly exceeded ours, yet our people drove them back with great loss, killing general Colbert, who commanded the advance. This was done by a noted pickle of the name of Tom Plunkett, who, fearless of all danger to himself, got sufficiently nigh to make sure of his mark, and shot him, which, with the fire of the others, caused great havoc in the enemy's ranks, and set them to flying to the rear much faster than they advanced......Cacabelos was distant from us only about a league.

Surtees states at the time, he was with Craufurd on his way to Vigo and in a different battalion. So his account can only have been produced from what he had heard. Kincaid repeats Plunkett's shooting of Colbert in his book(s) but at the time he was not even a Rifleman, and still a serving Militia officer. Therefore, again his account was hearsay. Captain Jonathan

---

[12] Kincaid describes Plunkett thus: 'A bold athletic Irishman, and a deadly shot; but the curse of his country was upon him, and I believe he was finally discharged, without receiving such a recompense as his merits in the field would otherwise secured to him.' Kincaid I believe had seen Costello's book or article to be able to comment on his pension details which we know not to be the case.

Leach makes no mention of Plunkett whatsoever in his extensive journals and neither does Bugler Green in his book, though both served in the 1st Battalion. Leach however, was not at Corunna. He had been left behind sick in Lisbon. Green was in Captain O'Hare's Company and therefore in the thick of the action so it is strange that he should omit such an important piece of regimental lore from his book.

Costello as we have seen was not at Corunna though of course knew of him while serving in the same battalion from 1809-1811. Costello and Plunkett were never in the same company, therefore, the only time Costello could observe Plunkett first-hand was when their respective companies were in action together or in camp. When Plunkett returned to the Peninsula with Captain Miller he was in a different battalion to Edward Costello, therefore at Waterloo they would not have had time to meet up. By the time Plunkett reached the Waterloo battlefield, Costello was already in Brussels wounded. Costello's account on arriving in Brussels and the chaos surrounding the numbers of wounded being brought into the city during his time there makes it highly unlikely that he would have come across Plunkett being treated (if he had been wounded) by a surgeon.

Cope and Verner, as far as I am aware used the same source material as I have but because they did not know the identity of the officer who wrote his personal account of Plunkett in the United Services journal 1842-43, chose to opt for Costello's version, which I have proved is flawed in parts. Captain George Miller is the only officer in the regiment who could have written to the United Service Journal who fits all aspects of his story. I have proved he was Plunkett's captain for the periods in question. Cope chose to use Miller's account of the South America incident in his history, for this is the only source material to give us the names of Plunkett and Fisher as being marksmen, the first time Plunkett's skill with the rifle is brought to our notice. Craufurd makes no mention of the shooting of the officer with a flag of truce in South America. In fact, quite the opposite - when an officer from General Liniers informs him of the fate of the other columns and asks for the surrender of his own force! Craufurd does make the case for the Riflemen that the defence of the convent was virtually all down to Mcleod's 1st Battalion Riflemen. If Plunkett did shoot and kill a previous officer with a flag of truce it is interesting that another was sent[13], and that later, when Craufurd surrendered, they were not treated the same and shot at, although Linier might have been tempered by the elation at having defeated such a strong British force. It is odd then that Cope and Verner chose *not* to use Miller's account of the shooting of Colbert. My firm belief is that Costello's hearsay version sounded the better of the two and what is more they wanted *that* version to be true! While I come down heavily in favour of Miller's version depicting the more believable scenario of events at Cacabelos, this being the only factual account, it is easy to see how the verbal account evolved over time with its constant retelling. The events surrounding Plunkett's shooting of Colbert, though obviously true, did not happen in the sequence given by Costello; Colbert on his grey horse, in Miller: Goulieu rode a white horse. The offer of monetary reward was for the shooting of the latter general, not Colbert. Plunkett did receive a gift of money along with a sergeant from Paget, but this was later in the retreat. We might have heard more about Plunkett from Captain Miller covering Waterloo, but unfortunately his

---

[13] Of course Plunkett could have shot the officer with the flag when he was returning to general Linier.

account in the United Service journal ends, leaving us no knowledge as to what he and Plunkett got up to at Waterloo and beyond. I am sure he would have written more for it is not only an account of Plunkett but also an insight into Miller's service. Shortly after Miller's last letter to the journal he died!

What has been lost in promoting Plunkett's inflated account of the shooting of General Colbert is the importance of the rear guard action at Cacabelos. The survival of Moore's army and it being able to fight a decisive battle on the 16th January 1809, was all down to their successful holding action and discipline, especially at Cacabelos and on the final retreat on Corunna. The Rifles part in this success can not be taken lightly or over stated especially when the casualties and missing are taken into account for the whole of the campaign. It is also interesting that in Rifle Green in the Peninsula volume one page 170 a list of Riflemen by company is shown who are all listed as being sick on returning to England. Some of these could be wounded but Captain Miller's company does not show Plunkett as sick or a casualty. Miller mentions Plunkett's slight wrist wound at Cacabelos but fails to enlighten us as to the more serious wound he was reported to have received at Waterloo, and the noticeable scar it left when they met up some years later. Miller goes to great lengths to tell us of the special relationship he and Plunkett formed, but this seems to have been based on purely a working one and did not extend into civilian life. If it had, I am sure he would have arranged some sort of employment for him. The volatile nature of his comrade especially around drink probably kept him at arms length.

 It would be interesting to hear from any reader who could offer any constructive views on my research or add to the debate on Plunkett, such as the observations on the Chichester angle. Much speculation has already been aired on the internet over the last ten years on Plunkett, covering the same old ground. The French have even entered the debate, though some of their offerings I discount, such as British officers paying their men to shoot French officers. The shooting of officers was not a new concept in the war against the French. The Royal Navy suffered such losses whenever their ships came into close-quarter battle, which of course resulted in the loss of the greatest ever British naval commander, Nelson at Trafalgar in 1805. They also give their version of events as to how Colbert met his death: "General Colbert fell during the second advance of the French cavalry after passing through or around the village (Cacabelos) and after seeing his aide shot on the other side of the river bank (eastern) having advanced as far as the lines of the skirmishers (British Riflemen) fell from a shot from the solid British entrenchments; the ball being fired by a Rifleman of the 95th, which struck him above the left eyebrow and passed through his head killing him instantly and throwing his body back off his horse." This account fits much more closely with Captain Miller's version than Costello's. The impact felt by Colbert was so strong that it killed him instantly and forced him backwards off his horse, suggests that his assailant was much closer than has been portrayed in most versions, especially the accounts that continue to extol the distance and difficulty of the shot. The illustration by Harry Payne which depicts Plunkett shooting Colbert has often been taken as an example of the true scenario because it mirrors Costello's version, and was probably reproduced from this description anyway. Again, it is only an artistic impression produced from a verbal description based on hearsay! Rutherford Moore says as much in his article though he attributes the illustration as being from the Rifle Brigade Chronicle journal for 1914. This is definitely not from this journal, it does however, appear in the 'Famous Regiments' series: *The Rifle Brigade* by Basil Harvey, and was photographed for the book by permission of the Green Jackets museum. It is up to the reader to assess the facts as I have presented them and to form their own opinion on the merit of my argument. In my mind I have no doubt that the events happened more or less as reported by Miller at Cacabelos and, until some new evidence is found to alter that thinking I feel we must take Costello's account as being correct in one fact only, "Plunkett shot Colbert!" At the same time we must be grateful for Costello's contribution, making Plunkett much more than just the man who shot Colbert, leaving us an insight into his complex character. Though a little sketchy in places much of what he tells us of him after Corunna fits in with the known facts supported in TNA and Miller's account.

Richard Rutherford-Moore, the arms consultant to the Sharpe series, says in an article, 'Recreating the 95th Rifleman,' that Plunkett married Elizabeth MacDermottroe an Irish girl, and after Tom's death she re-married in America giving birth to several children. If this can be corroborated then we have to question Mrs Plunkett's age! In 1815, when Costello informs us that she was disfigured by the explosion one would assume she was at least sixteen years of age? Costello was a Yeoman Warder in 1838 and his writings were first serialised in 1839, therefore, Mrs Plunkett would be nearing her forties when she confronted him at the Tower. If she visited Costello any later, then time is starting to go against her having a number of children, though not impossible of course as she seems to be a strong, sturdy character. If her facial injuries are correct, they obviously did not deter her second husband, while her ability at earning a living might have played a part here? Richard Rutherford Moore further states that Mrs Plunkett, having married and moved to America has descendents living there still to this very day. If any should ever read this book it would

71

be nice to hear their side of this conundrum. Richard also researched Plunkett's shot, having scoured what was left of the original battle site, his conclusion was that Plunkett did not make a shot of any considerable distance or difficulty, and that it was more likely to have been in the region of 100 yards, with which I agree after examining the incident as previously detailed in these pages.

The American Magazine 'Guns and Ammo' in the 1980's, completed a test firing of 25 rounds at a silhouette target at a distance of 100 yards with a baker rifle made and dated 1809, with not a single miss fire from a single flint. They had cast the rounds from lead as the originals would have been, and tied a few up in 0.010 inch thick ticking. The others were left naked, to be loaded with Ox-Yoke Originals 0.010 pre-lubricated patches. The rifle was used in conjunction with an original powder-horn of the Duke of Northumberland Rifles, complete with integral Irish-style powder measure that held 110 grains of F.F.g black powder. Having loaded the rifle with 110 grains powder and a patch ball, they primed the pan from a smaller flask with F.F.g powder. The recoil of the rifle was not prohibitive but from a rest position the small projection on the butt box had a tendency to dig into the collar bone. Lock time, whilst not instantaneous, was at least reasonably fast for a military arm. When the smoke cleared there was a hole in the upper left corner of the target paper. The next round struck the silhouette's torso in the eight ring and the third round missed the board altogether. In fact, it took 17 shots to get 10 rounds on the target. The extreme spread was about three and a half feet, duplicating almost exactly the test results of Baker, the rifles maker, in his test firing! Two of the bullets fired were the ones previously tied up in ticking as per the period cartridge round. They fared little better than the balls shot with loose patches.

72

One hit the target in the head region and the other missed the board completely.

It is surprising to see it took seventeen shots to put ten rounds on target from an accurate weapon and one wonders how the musket would have compared under the same kind of testing. The details reported in the American test firing are most welcome and bring home to the reader what was involved in making exceptional shots, highlighting what skill men like Plunkett exhibited at this period in British warfare. At the same time one must take into consideration that their testing and that of Baker were undertaken at leisure, without being fired upon themselves, with the firer being well fed, pretty healthy, relaxed and probably enjoying reasonably good weather conditions.

At present the mystery still remains as to the date Tom died and where his last resting place is. This seems to be against it being Colchester. We have yet to establish where Captain George Miller's French General, Goulieu fits into this research as there is no evidence at present to suggest he ever existed!

However, Captain George Miller leaves us with one final anecdote that probably sums up Plunkett's character and what endeared him to so many of his comrades. How truthful this is, is questionable for the simple reason Miller could not have been witness to the event, for it happened between 1809 and 1811. Miller was not with the 1st Battalion 95th Rifles during this period, therefore he had to have been told of the incident. It also tells us that Plunkett was the possessor of a quick thinking mind and had the wit to assess a situation and turn it to his advantage, which on this occasion saved him from what could have been a most serious situation with the unpredictable General Craufurd;

he was certainly an out and out rascal.

"I was informed that Plunkett killed another general, and no doubt put his mark upon many others. One day he happened to be trudging' along the road, with a pig in a string behind him, when as bad luck would have it, who should overtake him but Bob Craufurd. The salutation, as may be supposed, was not the most cordial.
'Where did you steal the pig, you plundering rascal?' Tom turning around to him with an air of surprise ... "What pig, Ginerl?" "What pig! why, that pig you have behind you, you villain you." Tom turning round to his friend, as if he had never seen him before,... "Well, I declare, Ginerl, some fellow, wanting to get me into trouble, has tied that *baste* to my cartouche box." The General could contain his risible faculties no longer, stuck spurs to his horse and rode on."

SERVICE HISTORY OF CAPTAIN
GEORGE MILLER C.B., 95th Rifles[14]

2nd Lieutenant	18 July 1804
Lieutenant	8 May 1805
Captain	21 January 1808
Brevet-Major	3 March 1814
Brevet-Lieutenant	
Colonel	18 June 1815
Major	23 December 1819
Lieutenant-Colonel unattached	25 May 1826

---

[14] Taken from the Rifle Brigade Century, an Alphabetical list of Officers 1800-1905 printed in 1905.

Colonel   10 January 1837

Died   20 November 1843

Taken prisoner at Buenos Aires, was in retreat and battle of Corunna, served in the Walcheren Expedition, also Barrosa, Badajoz, St. Sebastian[15] Pyrenees, Orthes, Tarbes where he was severely wounded. He returned to the Pyrenees 30 August 1812, was wounded at the Battle of Waterloo when in command of number One company 2nd battalion 95th Rifles. Made a C.B. and received Gold Medal for Nivelle and medal for Waterloo. To have received a Gold medal for Nivelle Miller had to be at that battle also.

---

[15] Miller was not at Badajoz or San Sebastian.

Bibliography

The National Archives;
WO/5419-5420; 9522-9525; 9577, 9584-9585; 10110;
11111; 11121 Regimental Muster rolls.
WO97/1085; WO120/30; WO12/5418

The Peninsula and Waterloo Campaigns Edward Costello,
London 1967 edited by Anthony Brett-James.

Royal United Services Institute Journals 1839-1843.

United Services Journal, June 1842-1843 Miller's account

Rifle Green in the Peninsula volumes One and Two George
Caldwell and Robert Cooper.   Bugle Horn Publications 1997
and 2007.

Rifle Green at Waterloo George Caldwell and Robert Cooper.
Bugle Horn Publications 1990.

*Observations on the exercise of Riflemen and on the movements
of Light Troops in general*, by Sergeant Weddeburne 95th Rifles
1804.

History of the Rifle Brigade W.Cope Chatto and Windus 1877
History and Campaigns of the Rifle Brigade Volumes One and
Two. Willoughby Verner London 1912-1919, reprinted 1996.

Recreating the 95th Rifleman Richard Rutherford-Moore

The Autobiography of Lieutenant-General Sir Harry Smith G.
Moore Smith 1901

Rough Sketches of the life of an old soldier Lieutenant-Colonel

J. Leach 1831, reprinted Ken Trotman 1986.

A Brief outline of the Travels and Adventures of William Green (Late Rifle Brigade)During a Period of ten years in the British Service 1857.

Where duty Calls me – The Experiences of William Green of Lutterworth in the Napoleonic Wars edited by John and Dorothea Teague, 1973.

Recollections of Rifleman Harris edited by Henry Curling 1848 and later editions.

A British Rifleman by George Simmons, edited by Willoughby Verner 1899 reprinted 1986.

The Adventures of a Soldier, or Memoirs of Edward Costello of the Rifle Brigade, Comprising Narratives of Wellington's Campaigns in the Peninsula, etc. Colbourne & Co, London, 1841. Second edition 1852.

Costello: The story of a Peninsular Rifleman Edited Eileen Hathaway 1997

TOM PLUNKET[16]

The following text is reproduced from The United Service Magazine 1842, Part II...

As you have given some interesting biographical sketches of distinguished military characters, may I claim a corner for an old comrade of mine — a hero of the first water. This is no less a personage than Tom Plunket, full private in H.M. ould (sic) 95th Regiment, a well-known character in the Light Division.
I shall therefore give you some account of his operations, as far as I happen to be acquainted with them, with some odds and ends as we go along, to connect the story; and if any of those are alive with whom he served, perhaps they may add another yarn to his adventures.

He was a native of a certain green isle in the west, the inhabitants of which are rather celebrated for their belligerent propensities; and if this be so, he was a true son of the sod. Fighting was his delight, and he was never so happy as when under fire. He was about the middle size, well-made, and active, capable of enduring great fatigue, and always in good humour even in the worst of times. He was not free from infirmities more than his neighbours: a platonic affection existed between him and the bottle; and, as frequently happens in this very indifferent world, his dearest friend now and then proved his bitterest enemy. Reckless being though he was, however, when under fire, he was the soberest and most cautious of riflemen. In choosing his ground, so as to cover himself and bring his fire to bear with the greatest effect upon the enemy, I never saw his equal: he always had his arms and ammunition in the nicest

---

[16] We have decided to retain the United Service Magazine spelling with of "t" for Plunkett

order; and sure it was himself that knew how to use them.

We set out on an expedition, in 1806, of 5000 men, under Colonel Craufurd, to circumnavigate the globe, and land on the western coast of South America. In the Bay of Biscay we had the usual adventures. When landsmen and young sailors first visit that portion of his dominions, Eolus is generally supposed to blow his bellows with more than usual violence. Be that as it may, he certainly gave us a puff extra, for we had fourteen days of it right on end, and no mistake. The wind, however, at last came fair, and we soon forgot our sorrows.

Sailed along the coast of Portugal with a flowing sheet; made the island of Madeira, where we laid in a stock of wine, to cheer us on our way. Passed the Canaries, where we saw, or fancied we saw, the lofty Peak, and shortly after cast anchor in Porto Praya harbour, in the Cape de Verd islands, where we remained a month. I have never been able to ascertain the cause of this delay: but, he that as it may, 1 have always considered this as one of the most pleasant months of my existence. The rapid transition from the wintry hills of England to perpetual spring, was quite enchanting. We made frequent excursions into the interior of the island, and found some of the valleys extremely beautiful. The land abounds with Guinea-fowl, and the sea is alive with fish, so that there was ample occupation for the sportsman.

One day, a ship near us hooked a huge shark, and, as the master of our vessel was passing at the time, a serjeant's halberd was handed down to him to finish the varmint. He, accordingly, thrust it right through his back, when the monster made a desperate effort, broke the line, and got clear off, halberd and all.

It was here that the well-known adventure occurred of Capt. King, of the Carabineers, going ashore with a sack, into which be intended to cram the Portuguese Governor, and sell him to a slaver, lying in the harbour. Fortunately the Governor's pistol missed fire, which prevented rather a tragical termination to the drama. But, as his Excellency was passing, a day or two afterwards, in his barge, the Captain shook the sack at him, to remind him of the compliment intended for him.

Thus passed the merry hours: "Youth at the prow, and Pleasure at the helm," Hope danced before us in all the gay colours of the rainbow. But, of all the merry hearts there assembled, how few remain!

Up anchor again, and, after a fortnight's broiling under the line, in a calm and rather a tedious passage, doubled the mighty Cape, and cast anchor in Simon's Bay. The roaring of the surf there, in a still night, is very grand. As our Admiral did not like his situation here altogether, he brought us round to Table Bay; and well it was that he did so, for a heavy gale came on shortly afterwards, which made the greater part of the fleet to drive. The decks of the ships were covered with dust upwards of a mile from shore, and a fleet of Chinamen, which attempted to enter the Bay, was obliged to bear away. One of them had to cut away her mizen-mast, and was very nearly wrecked. During the short time we remained here, I visited Constantia and as much of the neighbourhood as the time permitted.

During the time we remained here it was rumoured that a brig-of-war had arrived from England, with orders to countermand the expedition, and proceed to the River Plate, to assist in the recapture of Buenos Ayres; and when we stood out of the bay all eyes were turned to watch the Admiral's signal for the course, which soon left no doubt upon the subject. We soon ran down to St. Helena, where we remained a week. I went ashore one day early to examine the island. Visited Longwood, —a place of some celebrity afterwards, —breakfasted with a black man upon boiled rice, and then pursued my journey. After some labour found myself perched on the highest pinnacle of rock, in the centre of the island, which commands a view all round. I had hardly finished my survey, however, when I was enveloped in a dense fog, which kept me a close prisoner while it lasted, in that very uncomfortable position. My captivity was not quite so long as that of Napoleon. It was sufficiently long, however, to enable me to sympathize with him in feelings on that subject; and the fog had no sooner cleared away than I made my escape from that lump of rock, —the most miserable habitation on the face of the earth.

Up anchor again, and stood across the Atlantic. Passed Fernando Noronha, cousin german to St. Helena, and, as we neared the coast of America, the wind became adverse, and we had a long and tedious passage up to the Plate. This we found by no means pleasant; for, after being so long at sea, our sea-stock failed us, and we were at last reduced to G R[17], as tough as shoe-leather, which was swallowed in sober silence by the long faces assembled round the dinner-table. Some slight symptoms of scurvy also began to appear among the troops. We at last go the anchor in the mouth of the Plate, however, and flattered ourselves that our watery troubles were near an end. In this, however, we were mistaken. A *pampero* came on in earnest, and burst like thunder over us. Our ship of 600 tons plunged bows under, the cables parted, and away we drove upwards of 100 miles before the storm. She had braved the

---

[17] General rations. Ed

winds and waves nearly half a century, (so report said,) but this night certainly threatened to terminate her career, ballasted with sand, and six feet water in the hold, the pumps choked every quarter of an hour, while the whole stern threatened to part company bodily. In those days, when a ship was no longer worthy to carry rum-puncheons and sugar-hogsheads from the West Indies, or coals from Newcastle to London, she was degraded to carry soldiers. If she went to the bottom the mishap was attributed to the weather, and that was all.

The fleet was completely dispersed; but the ships found their way singly up to Monte Video, where 8000 men at least assembled, of the finest troops that ever left England, under the command of General Whitelocke, a man well known to history. This General was what, in military parlance, is termed a smart officer, a great martinet, a great favourite at the Horse Guards, and the terror of all subs, particularly when upon guard. Then who so fit to command as General Whitelocke?

The troops were removed from the larger vessels and packed into the smaller ones, something like herrings into a barrel. When one half lay down, the other half found it convenient to stand. The officers swung in the cabin in three tiers, like chests of drawers. I happened to swing in the middle, and the man who slept below me adopted the precaution of fixing a preventer brace round my cot during the night, lest I should bring up on the top of him before morning, and then lay down on the cabin floor, to lament his hard luck and the cruel position in which he was placed. The passage up the river was pleasant. The troops at this time had cocoa for breakfast, and one morning, when on duty, the serjeant of the watch came to me, and touching his cap very gracefully, notified that the water was fresh, and asked permission to make the men's breakfast from the river, which was granted accordingly. The serjeant was mistaken, however; the water was not fresh, and caused no small commotion in the ship, attended with no more serious consequences, however, than a hearty laugh at my expense. I was gravely told that I had acted rashly, as no one under the rank of a general doctor had any right to administer a general purge.

Anchored at Colonia, where we took in some troops that were there, and then stood across the river, which is there thirty miles broad, and landed at *Ensenada de Barragan*, or the bay of Barragan, about thirty miles below Buenos Ayres, where we bivouacked for the night. Just before our arrival, a tiger had come out of the reeds by the river side and killed a horse; he was shot by a Spaniard, who cut off his head and placed it on a pole. The ghost of the tiger kept our sentinels particularly alert during the night.

The advanced guard, under General Gore, consisted of 1200 men, one half riflemen, and the other half light infantry. Our line of march next day lay through a bog of several miles, up to the knees in mud. About the middle of this, I came rather abruptly upon an animal, something like a good-sized pig; he manifested no symptoms of retreat, but raising himself upon his hinder parts, and showing his tusks, told me in very plain terms that I was an intruder. I admitted the justice of his claim, made a flank movement, and left him in undisturbed possession of his domain.

It was amusing to see the soldiers, from time to time, thrusting their arms into the mud up to the shoulder, fishing for shoes that had parted company. Let me recommend this promenade to all keen Nimrods who go to foreign parts in search of feathered fowls; if game is as abundant now as it was then, they will not be disappointed, from an ostrich down to a snipe. When we got to *terra firma,* a few mounted skirmishers made their appearance, who, dismounting occasionally, fired their long guns over their saddles, at an awful distance. The country was covered with thousands of cattle. In the evening, a drove of them came to reconnoitre us; but whether from curiosity, or with hostile intentions, I cannot exactly say. It was deemed advisable, however, to fire a few shots at them, by way of admonition.

We halted in a comfortable farm-house for the night, which contained nothing but a magnificent stock of poultry, not one of which lived to see the morning light. I was amused this evening with two Spaniards catching a wild horse. They drove him into a bog, where he stuck. One of them then advanced upon firm ground, threw a noose over his head, and running it tight, almost strangled him, while the other put a powerful bridle in his mouth, and led him off in triumph.

This evening a deserter came over to us in the shape of a big dog. He kept watch and ward upon the outposts, and the soldiers said, was equal to half-a-dozen of them. As may be supposed, he became a great favourite during the short time that our acquaintance lasted.

Next morning I went out with a few men, and shot a bullock. Dragged him home with a horse in triumph, and cut him up. This was the most substantial bit of game I ever bagged.

Next day the enemy's skirmishers were rather more numerous, but did no execution. Passed a hamlet in flames; and arrived in the evening at no great distance from Buenos Ayres, but the river, which surrounds the city on the south and east, ran between us. There was much platoon firing in the city towards sunset, the note of preparation.

We were quartered in a comfortable farm-house; and mine host, to his other avocations, seemed to add that of apothecary, for he had a tolerable laboratory as far as bottles went. In overhauling his stock in trade, which occupied me a considerable part of the night, I at last stumbled upon a bottle of wine, which I discussed instanter. I had no sooner done so, however, than I fancied myself poisoned; and with that dismal impression upon my mind, I fell fast asleep in his great leathern arm-chair, and slept soundly until the dawn of day.

During the night, one of the enemy's skirmishers led his horse slanting, keeping himself on the offside between two sentinels, and passed unnoticed. He then remounted, rode handsomely into the very centre of our picket, around the watchfire in the middle of the court-yard, and got clear off before the alarm could be given. He did it neatly, and we gave him credit for his adroitness.

The order was to march next morning at seven o'clock in the morning; and march we did accordingly at that hour; but his Excellency General Whitelock did not move with the main body of the army until a considerable time afterwards. The communication was thus lost, and this was blunder the first in this comedy of errors. Our General, however, bowled along, determined to carry all before him; and he would have done so, if he had only kept the steam up. When we came opposite the bridge leading across the river to the city, we found the whole Spanish army in position on the side of it, with a powerful artillery. About 200 cavalry formed line in front of it, and seemed disposed to fight; but a few shots from our guns sent them across the bridge; for we had two 6-pounders worked by seamen, who enjoyed the fun exceedingly. I observed one of them with seven canteens slung round him: he looked like the planet Saturn, with his seven satellites.

As it was deemed advisable not to disturb the Spaniards in their beautiful position, we pursued our march parallel to the right bank of the river. When General Liniers, the governor, saw this, he took 5000 of his best troops, and endeavoured to march parallel to us, on his side of the river; but we outmarched him, and forded the river breast-high, about four miles above the city, and then marched directly upon it. The enemy's skirmishers then became more numerous, but still kept at a respectful distance. A man of the name of Fraser, however, tumbled one of them at a long shot. He passed the body unnoticed; but one of those who came after undid his sash, in which he found fifty-two doubloons. At a subsequent period our soldiers had much greater curiosity in overhauling a Frenchman's wallet, and seldom made mistakes of that kind.

Liniers finding that we had crossed the river, turned to his right, and posted his troops on an eminence, about a mile from the city, with sixteen or seventeen pieces of artillery, where he awaited our approach. We advanced upon him in skirmishing order, the lofty prickly-pear hedges concealing us, until we were close upon the enemy. As soon as we opened our fire, they made but a feeble resistance, fired off their guns, and took to their heels, leaving their guns behind them, and a number of gaily embroidered caps, very much in the shape of a frying pan. There were very few killed or wounded in this battle, but a great many frightened. We followed them up close, and placed two companies in the houses at the corners of two cross streets, at the entrance of the city, while I was pushed on with a few men, about 300 yards down the main street.

This was the golden opportunity. I afterwards met with General Balbiani in Spain, the second in command, who informed me that we had only to send in a summons, and all was over. On what trivial circumstances do great events sometimes depend! Upon this occasion, the blast of a trumpet would have subdued a city, conquered a province, and saved the lives of thousands; but the lungs to blow the trumpet were wanting.

Night had now closed in; and; shortly after, I was surprised to find the Field Officer of the day come up to me, and tell me, that the piquets were about to retire, and that I was to follow their movements. When I approached the houses where they had been posted, I observed a stout, or rather corpulent, person come out of one of them, dressed in plain clothes. As he was moving along the cross street, at right angles to the direction I was approaching him, he kept looking after the piquets, muttering to himself. I called out to him to surrender; upon which he took to his heels. Had I been fresh, I could easily have caught him; but, having been three nights on piquet, and in my wet clothes, I was not in a condition to follow him. I made the men that were with me fire after him; but in the dark they missed him.

This was Liniers himself, who thus had a very narrow escape; and, having discovered our plan of retiring, he did not fail to take advantage of it. In a very short space of time, the main street was lighted up from end to end, and a party of cavalry came along the cross street, upon which I fired, and drove them back. We then retired about a mile, where we remained under arms. During the night, the whole of the Spanish army was brought back into the city; the streets were cut and planted with cannon, houses loopholed, and every preparation made for defence. A heavy fall of rain raised the river, and prevented the main body of our army from crossing for two days. This gave the enemy time to complete his arrangements. Next morning, we again pushed forward our skirmishers. In advancing, we found another heavy gun, which the enemy had abandoned the preceding evening. Lieut. Mac—[18], from the sister isle, said that he understood engineering, and volunteered his services to spike it; but, as it happened to be loaded, in the act of hammering it exploded, and the wheel running over the engineer's big toe, gave him a place among the honourable list of wounded.

We now found the enemy occupying the suburbs in great force; and, in the three days' skirmishing which ensued, it was surprising with what rapidity their confidence increased. I never saw the French shoot so well as they did. Any one exposed for a single minute, at a range of two hundred yards, had no chance of escape whatever. On one occasion, our light infantry got the worst of it, in fair skirmishing, and had to be supported. This certainly arose from no inferiority in the troops, for a great portion of those opposed to them were slaves, but from an inferiority of fire.

Will John Bull never learn, that the most ill-judged economy that ever was thought of, is that of giving inferior arms to troops? Joseph Hume, himself, upon the score of profit and loss, would cry—Shame at such a system! And it may naturally be asked—How comes it, that a nation which manufactures the best arms in the world, should supply her troops with those of the very worst description? The answer is easy: the small-arm department is under the control of a Woolwich Committee, men

---

[18] This is more than likely to be Lieutenant MacNamara. Ed

half a century behind the age in which they live. There are many intelligent officers in the Ordnance department, but, somehow or other, they seem to have no say in the matter, not being qualified by anility for that important duty. Surely these things ought not to be. With such arms and ammunition as this country could have supplied, I believe that the Duke of Wellington might have accomplished all that he did with half his numbers. Some improvement is now threatened; but it is not what it ought to be.

A feigned retreat was attempted, to draw the enemy from the city; but it failed to do so. One of them was so indignant at being taken prisoner, that he took a flying leap down a deep well, where his bones may possibly still remain.

At last an attack was made upon the city, in four columns, at daybreak, leaving very little reserve. Our column was the second from the right, under Colonel Craufurd. We passed to the right of the city; and then turning sharply to the left, crossed it, and took possession of the convent of San Domingo, near the banks of the Plate. We met with no opposition in our advance, unless in crossing the main street, down which the enemy kept up an incessant fire of grape; but we ran across in small parties without loss. We were not attacked for a considerable time; but at last, when the two left columns were overpowered, the enemy bore down upon us in great force, occupying all the streets and houses around us. The houses are particularly well adapted for defence, being substantially built, and grated in lower windows, with flat roofs and parapets.

Plunket, and a man of the name of Fisher, were hoisted upon the roof of a low building, adjoining the church, and commanding the principal street leading to it, where those two gallant fellows continued to fire for hours. The shot flew about them like hail; but they kept bobbing their heads from time to time, and, strange to say, escaped untouched.

At last, Liniers sent a flag of truce by his aide-de-camp, to summon us to surrender. Plunket, who did not know much about flags of truce at that time, said, "I'll have a slap at the fellow with the white handkerchief." He shot him through both thighs, of which he died three days afterwards. This was the greatest blot in Tom's escutcheon. The Spaniards cried "Shame!" and called us a barbarous people. It appeared to us at the time, however, that their principal object in sending a flag of truce was to get an opportunity of closing in more upon us. I lately asked Tom, when I met him in London, how many he thought he killed there. "I think I killed about twenty, Sir: I shot a gentleman with a flag of truce, Sir."

The enemy brought some heavy guns to bear upon the dome of the church, for the purpose of battering it down, and letting it fall through the roof upon us. A company of grenadiers was then sent out, under the gallant Major Trotter, to endeavour to force the passage for a retreat. I stood by the gate as that brave man went to destruction. He looked desponding for the first time in his life. They went out eighty-four, and returned in a few minutes twenty-three. I have never seen a more wanton sacrifice of human life. Ammunition began to fail, —a common occurrence in a British army; a council of war was held, and it was agreed to surrender.

I could never see the necessity of this measure. Night was not far off; we might have held on until dark, and then forced our way out, though, no doubt, with loss.

Thus ended the attack on Buenos Ayres, one of the most disgraceful events in the annals of England, three columns out of four being either killed or taken prisoners. But even in these desperate circumstances, a resolute man would by no means have given all up for lost, and agreed to evacuate the country. One column did not surrender; the cavalry were armed with muskets, and in reserve, and the 87th Regiment had stormed and captured the Retira, or Bull Fight, in gallant style, with a loss of 350 men [The 87th Regiment was nearly all cut to pieces in the attempt, and the position, if we are not greatly mistaken, was carried by the 38th Regiment.—ED.] This was by far the most commanding position in the neighbourhood, —a fortress in itself, and it secured the communication with the shipping. Had this been taken in the first instance, without entering the city, there can be little doubt that it would at once have surrendered. The enemy seemed evidently to expect this, for he had garrisoned it strongly, and placed the greater part of his artillery there. It might have been held against any numbers of the enemy, and, even supposing the worst, the remaining troops might have been embarked and landed at Montevideo, where Lord Blayney arrived shortly afterwards with 1500 men. In fact, there was only one way of losing the place, and that was the one adopted.

After surrendering, Liniers received the officers in the street courteously enough. We were then marched into the citadel, where a hundred and five of us were crammed into two rooms, leading into each other, —a motley group, sure enough, and we certainly looked monstrous queer. The first day we had little or nothing to eat, but a tub of water was placed in the outer apartment, the object of which was not exactly understood by all. Some went to drink, some went to p—, and some went to drink again. The inner room was made the sleeping one, where each occupied as many bricks as his body covered, and no

92

more. We lay down, not quite sure whether our throats would be cut during the night or not. Towards morning all the drinkers No.3, of which I was one, were seized with a certain laxity of bowels, which was anything but agreeable. As my lair was next the wall I had to thread my way through the carpet of legs and arms, which I did as carefully as I could, but finding that I was about to lose my balance, I was obliged to make a fair run through them. When I got near the outside I observed something of a lighter colour, which I took to be firm footing. Made a spring, and got upon it sure enough. It proved to be a gentleman's white waistcoat, who was fast asleep on the broad of his back. The wind went out of him, like the squeeze of a piper's bag, and the whole room was presently in an uproar, everyone calling out, "What's the matter, —what's the matter?" "Oh, that officer, that d—d Rifle officer has made a ab—ord of me." When I got to the place of retirement I found myself followed by Major, since General Macleod, who requested, as a particular favour, my turn of duty, as his claims were of the most urgent nature. I was in no haste to return, as I calculated that my friend's steam would be up, —he of the white waistcoat, —and no apology could atone for so grievous an offence. I was afterwards informed that he drew his sword, one of the few left in the party, and swore that he would cut anyone down who came within arm's length of him. If the gentleman is still alive, I sincerely beg his pardon.

Next morning our gun-boats stood in, and opened their fire on the very spot where we were confined, and sent a 24-pounder into the next room to us. The Spaniards manned their batteries, under the direction of a priest, and looked particularly sulky. The evacuation of the country having been agreed to, our release followed accordingly. When we marched out of prison it was discovered that one of the party, by the fortune of war, had marched into a pair of priest's breeches. He looked very uncomfortable; and for this act of sacrilege, to protect both, him and ourselves from insult, or something worse, it was deemed prudent to form a *cordon sanitaire* around him. We passed heaps of our own dead, all stripped and unburied. When we arrived at the Retiro, the first person we met was General Whitelocke. "Gentlemen," said he, "I am glad to see so many green-jackets together again. I can assure you I have had much uneasiness on your account, for I expected that fellow Liniers to put you all to death." To this speech no answer was returned. When we got to Montevideo we thought ourselves very unlucky in not getting a ship called the Alexander, which foundered on the Western Isles. On leaving the river we had one of those tremendous gales to which that country is subject. Next morning I happened to be on duty, when the Master came on deck at daybreak, and asked where the fleet was. As I knew that we were in a good ship, I replied it was to leeward. He accordingly put up his helm, and ran before the storm, and after looking out for the fleet two days in vain, opened his instructions, and stood for Portsmouth, where we arrived about ten days before the fleet.

Tom's next adventures were in Spain. We landed at Corunna, under Sir David Baird, and advanced to Astorga smoothly enough, while Sir John Moore advanced from Lisbon to Salamanca. But bad news now came thick upon us, in the dispersion of the Spanish armies, and the advance of Napoleon to Madrid with a powerful reinforcement.

While the troops were assembling at Astorga I was sent on to Benavente, to keep a look-out, and gain intelligence of the enemy. Upon my return to Astorga, among other things it was reported that the French were advancing along the coast of

Asturias, to get into our rear; upon which Sir David desired me to post there, and see if it was so. I accordingly set out immediately, reached Leon about midnight, and having a letter to the Marquis of Romana, who was at the Bishop's palace, I went there to rap him up. After thundering at the door for some time I was admitted by a man with a huge lantern, to whom I told my errand. He led me through several gloomy chambers, and we at last reached the Marquis's bedroom. He was fast asleep in the corner of it, upon a common Spanish bed, without curtains. Upon my entering he started up in his red night-cap, and seemed to think his murderers at hand. I advanced quietly to his bedside, and told my story. He seemed in very low spirits, said but little, countersigned my passport, and addressed himself again to sleep, while I pursued my journey. At the magnificent pass of Pajaris I met a considerable body of his troops, returning from the defeat of Reymosa. The commanding officer detained me a considerable time, and insisted that I must be French, notwithstanding my passport and protestations to the contrary. He at last suffered me to depart, minus my pistols, however, which his faithful followers had borrowed in the meantime. What thieves those Spaniards are! Several of the stragglers seemed very well disposed to give me the benefit of a shot. Among others, I passed several cavalry officers that we had entertained at Falmouth, on their return from the Baltic, drinking success to the Spanish cause, and expecting soon to clear the Peninsula of the enemy. Our prospects were not now quite so bright.

At Oviedo I spent two or three days very agreeably, visiting Gigon and the neighbourhood. One of the best houses in the Plaza was appropriated to the use of the English,—an Englishman being then a curiosity. Finding that the French were not advancing I rode onto meet them. Visited the celebrated oak of Guernica, under which the Kings of Spain, as *Lords of Biscay,* swore to maintain the *Fueros* of Biscay, and well would it have been for Spain if that ceremony had been continued. This tree is surrounded by an iron railing, and well preserved.

I fell in with the enemy at the Pass of Colombres, where Ballasteros commanded on his side of the valley. His troops were of the Falstaff school, and the evening of my arrival I was called on to assist at a council of war, about midnight, to consider the plan of operations; when it was agreed to hold on until obliged to do otherwise.

I at once saw that the French had no intention of offensive operations there at that time, as they had only a weak battalion on their side of the valley which they marched daily round the opposite hill, turning their jackets at the back of it, marching round a second time in their new garb; again countermarching the jackets, and marching round a third time. They thus appeared three times more numerous than they really were. Ballasteros did not like this gasconade, and got up a 9-pounder one night, which he opened upon them next day in the midst of their march. None of the shot struck the column, but it made them scamper, and they did not repeat the promenade.

Upon my return from Infiesto I made a detour to the south of several leagues, into the mountains, where I halted at a small village for the night. The people seemed courteous enough; but in the evening the wise men of the place came into my apartment, I at first thought to pay their respects to me, but none of the usual empty compliments following, I began to suspect their taciturnity. Having seated themselves, they held a council of war, to decide whether or not they should put me to death for being a Frenchman. The English army, they said, was dressed in scarlet,—I was not so, —and that was proof positive. An

96

interpreter was called in, —a soldier who had been a prisoner on board the hulks at Portsmouth, where he had learned English. His vocabulary consisted of three words, *salt, bread,* and *water,* which I was called upon to translate in due form. Having rung the changes upon them some fifty times, and displayed his lore to his wondering countrymen, he at last gave it as his opinion that I was English, from my pronunciation. I felt much obliged to the honest man; but as I did not like my situation much, I hauled on my breeches next morning long before cock-crowing, and marched off without beat of drum, escorted by a soldier, however, back to Infiesto, to make sure that I was not an impostor. The road was beautifully garnished with crosses, emblems of so many murders. Mine host there received me with his former kindness; and having passed the night with him I proceeded on to Oviedo, where I found an order to rejoin the army, about to advance.

I accordingly started a little before sunset, and spent one of the most dreary nights I ever passed in my life in crossing the mountain-range between Asturias and Leon. The weather was bitter cold, and the road covered with ice and snow. I did not meet a human being except at the post-houses. The wolves, however, kept me company, sometimes trotting before me along the road; and, as they seemed to be looking out for their supper, I did not much like their familiarity.

Next day I dined with the Bishop of Leon and his monks,—a sombre party enough, —and started again in the evening. It is a posting rule in Spain that if the traveller rides behind the postilion, and the horse dies from fatigue, he is set free; but if he rides first he has to pay for him. To guard against this accident I always took care to select the better horse for myself, putting my companion in front, with a good whip behind him, to keep him in his relative position. Unfortunately, as the night was very dark, a certain application of it sent both Sancho and Rosinante, head over heels into a deep ditch by the roadside. I thought there was an end of both; but after a dead silence for some time, the doleful accents at last issued from the ditch, which sounded music in mine ears, *0 Senor roriz tripas*! After a while, I got them both on end again, and we jogged on to the end of the stage, where it is to be hoped the *tripas* recovered their wonted tone.

I found Sir D. Baird at Benavente, sitting over a glass of mulled wine, with his Staff. There had been considerable vacillation in my absence. The army had retired, and again advanced. He told me it was to advance the following day, but seemed to have no great confidence in the movement; for he said, among other things, "I'm glad that the responsibility is off my shoulders. In fact, Sir J. Moore seems to have been driven to this unhappy movement by the importunities of Mr. Frere."

We crossed the Eslar below Benavente, and advanced by Mayorga towards Sahagun. As we approached the latter place, we heard that our cavalry had had a brilliant affair with that of the enemy, and were of course anxious to learn particulars. Our Assistant-Surgeon happening to meet a Serjeant returning, accosted him, "Well, Serjeant, how was it?" "I declare," said the man of stripes, "they were seventeen deep, Sir; I thought that I should never have cut through them."

We halted a day at Sahagun, and marched the following evening to attack Soult, who was posted on the Carrion. But when within a short distance of him, advices arrived to say, that Napoleon was not far off, advancing from Madrid by forced marches upon our rear. Countermarch then was the word; and we had a fair race of 270 miles to Corunna. We had just time to cross the Eslar, when Napoleon's advanced guard appeared. A detachment of ours was left to break down the bridge; and there was some skirmishing during the night. Next day there was a false alarm at Benavente, that the enemy had entered the town, which caused some confusion. Next morning, Napoleon came up with his Staff to the heights above the bridge, whilst his guards tried the depth of the river at various parts. Having found a ford, they crossed over under Lefebvre. They were immediately attacked in the plain by our cavalry, who routed them, taking Lefebvre and many more prisoners. As he passed us, I observed that he had a very ugly sabre cut in the face, but seemed nowise dejected. It was said that he expected to be retaken. His companions, ploughing through the mud in their crimson pantaloons, looked sober enough.

At Astorga the quantity of stores of all kinds that was destroyed, was immense; and to increase the confusion, Romana's troops had arrived there. Hardly any rations were served out to the troops after this, and the disorganization of the Army began in earnest.

At Calcabalos, plunder being the order of the day, Sir John Moore formed the troops into square, and told them, among other things, "Soldiers, if you do not behave better, I would rather be a shoe-black than your General." These were the last words I ever heard him utter. Next day, matters not being mended, the troops were again formed into square, while three delinquents were hoisted upon men's shoulders, with the ropes round their necks, to be suspended from the boughs of trees, when an officer (Capt. Ross,) rode in from the outposts, to say that the enemy was close at hand. Instead of hanging, it was then necessary to prepare for shooting. The troops were moved through the town without delay, but not before half of one of our companies were taken prisoners by the enemy's cavalry. Our brigade was then placed in the vineyards on the face of the opposite hill, one of the best positions which the whole line of retreat afforded. But they were hardly in position, when the two other regiments were retired, leaving our battalion, with two guns, to the tender mercies of some 3000 or 4000 Frenchmen, with that most delightful of all orders, *to hold on to the last* [19], to allow time for the evacuation of Villafranca, which was not far off.

Plunket was at this time going to the rear sick in an hospital waggon; but as soon as he heard that there was to be a fight, his sickness left him. He got hold of his rifle, stole out in the rear of the waggon, without the Doctor's knowledge, joined his company, and posted himself by the great road, when he was sure to be in the thick of it.

The enemy having made his disposition for attack, advanced in a dense column of cavalry and infantry, along the great road. As soon as they debouched from the town, our guns opened upon them. They advanced steadily however, until about half way up the hill, when a Shrapnell shell bursting in the centre of the column, made a lane completely through them. This staggered them for the moment, and brought them to a stand. Volunteers then, as they appeared to us, rode out from different parts of the column, and formed at the head of it: there might be about forty of them. They then advanced at speed, headed by Generals

---

[19] An officer of ours was once placed on picket in Portugal by the Major, with orders not to retire, *while he had a man left.* Upon which the other gravely asked him, "Whither then, Sir, shall I retire, in subdivisions or sections ?"

Colbert and Goulieu, to capture our guns, which limbered up and retired. The gallant cavaliers, however, passed through between us; and I never saw men ride more handsomely to destruction. Had Shakespeare seen them, he certainly would have classed them with those with whom time gallops withal. My company was on the left of the road, and two more on the right of it. We poured it into them right and left, and they went down like clockwork. Goulieu, who was mounted on a capital white charger, was particularly conspicuous. Lord Lyndoch called out, "I'll give any man two guineas to shoot the fellow on the white horse!—any man two guineas to shoot the fellow on the white horse!" "Please your Honor," said Plunket, who had just shot General Colbert, *"it won't cost you a tester."* He missed him, however, as did many others. The fellow on the while horse rode the gauntlet most gallantly, and got clear off, but I rather think he was the only one that did so.

Lieutenant Layton, as gallant a soldier as Plunket himself, jumped upon a Frenchman's horse, of which he was not a little proud. He had but a short ride, however, for Plunket observing the Imperial eagle on the saddle-cloth through the smoke, had an idea that he must be French, and as the horse and rider generally belong to the same nation, he thought them fairly entitled to the benefit of a shot. He fortunately missed Layton, but shot the horse dead. "The fellow," said Layton to me afterwards, "he shot my horse." I told him he might think himself particularly fortunate in not being shot himself, which was certainly intended.

During the action, I observed that Plunket had a shot through the sleeve of his coat. He was slightly wounded in the wrist, but said nothing about it, and continued at his post. After this, the enemy sent out clouds of skirmishers, round both rear and flanks, among others, Goulieu's dismountable cavalry, and pressed us hard indeed. We lost one hundred and twenty men that day, and had not night come to our assistance, we should have fared much worse.

Plunket was made a serjeant for his gallant conduct.

As we passed through Villafranca, several houses were in flames, and much confusion prevailed. Goulieu followed us up closely. His cavalry were certainly the most efficient I have ever seen. The British cavalry are now also taught to act on foot; at least we are told so; but they never seem to take to it kindly. A British dragoon when placed upon his mother earth, looks very much like a fish out of water. He seems half ashamed of the pedestals that nature gave him; and to think that the only legitimate way of overcoming an enemy, is either by riding him fairly down, or by cleaving him handsomely in twain from top to bottom.

The march from Bimbimbre was disorder personified. Four hundred men were left there intoxicated, and I think we must have lost ten or twelve hundred stragglers that day. The French advanced guard did not secure them, but passed on, so that friends and foes got blended together, forming only one column, and seeming to have the same object in view. Numbers were sitting by the roadside never to rise again. Among others, I remember a poor Highland recruit, completely knocked up, but retaining every article belonging to him. Upon being asked why he did not throwaway his musket, "Ah, Sir," said he, "the Colonel would be angry." It was broken to pieces, and his knapsack taken from him, but it was too late, nature was exhausted. It would be an instructive document, if it were possible to ascertain it, to know how many men we lost during the Peninsular war, *solely* from the enormous load they have to carry. I do not think it could be less than fifteen thousand.

Next day, as we were marching along the side of a hill, my company happening to be in the rear with a few dragoons, I observed a sort of scramble in the column before me. When I came up, I found it to be several car loads of money standing in the middle of the road, the bullocks that drew them being completely knocked up. Both officers and soldiers were helping themselves very freely to bags of dollars, which was certainly better than letting them fall into the hands of the enemy. They only got a small portion, however, for Goulieu, who was close behind us, as soon as he observed what was passing, sounded a charge, which made us take to our heels. There being a steep bank on our left, and a deep ravine on our right, we had to run a little way before we got out of the road, to fire down upon him, according to the custom of war in like cases. We then placed ourselves at a turn of the road behind some stone walls which covered us completely.

Goulieu halted his column to plunder the money, while he himself rode on a little in front to water his horse by the roadside, which brought him within about one hundred yards of us. The opportunity was not to be lost. I got hold of a rifle, and my officers did the same, to have a go at our tormentor. My gun flashed in the pan, and I shall probably never have such another opportunity of smiting a General. Before I got my touch-hole cleared, a man of the name of Matthews, standing by me, had floored him. He shot him right through the body, and the gallant fellow fell dead from his horse.

Here let me warn all bold dragoons to beware of white chargers. They look very pretty in a picture, or at a review in Hyde Park, to show off before the ladies, but they are dangerous cattle in the field.

103

We saw the horse afterwards, but the rider was a prudent person, and did not come quite so near us.

After the death of General Goulieu, the pursuit was not pressed with so much vigour. Plunket was very often absent from his company; but when a shot was fired, he very soon made his appearance. He supplied me tolerably well with provisions; and in those days of starvation, I never had the curiosity to ask him where he got them.

The number of dead horses was very great along the line of retreat; but as we approached Lugo, it was frightful. As soon as one knocked up, either from loss of shoes, or want of food, a pistol was put to his head; and it was painful to see the poor animal with the blood streaming from him until he fell to rise no more. At Lugo, our battalion was quartered in a rich nunnery, the hospitality of whose inmates I had formerly experienced. As I happened to be in the room where their papers were kept, tired though I was, such is the impulse of curiosity, that I passed a considerable part of the night in reading their letters,—rather a breach of good manners, perhaps; but so it was. I had a desire to learn the opinion of things in general, of those who lived on the world, but not in it. They had of course fled, and I dare say were very glad to regain their liberty. I have questioned many of the sisterhood on that point, and am led to that opinion.

Now that Lord Brougham and Co. have emancipated *Blacky,* it is to be hoped that they may turn their attention to the fair damsels immured in England.

There was a good deal of skirmishing at Lugo. The army was placed in position, and battle offered to the enemy, which he declined, at which I for one was not at all sorry, for our position appeared to me to be by no means a good one.

The evening that we retired, our Quartermaster was left behind for a short time, on some duty or other, so that when he came to move, he walked right into a French regiment. Retaining his presence of mind, however, he posted himself on the flank of a section;—and though a sturdy Highlander, passed for as good a Frenchman as any of them. Fortunately for him, the night was dark and stormy, so that his companions were as little disposed to talk as himself; and drawing his great-coat well over his face, he passed unnoticed. Towards morning he stole away; and floating himself across a river in a hog-trough, rejoined his regiment.

One day as the enemy was pressing us rather closely, Plunket and a Serjeant concealed themselves in a copse by the roadside, where they quietly awaited the approach of the head of the enemy's advanced guard, consisting of four men. They both fired, and emptied a couple of saddles. That trifling circumstance checked the pursuit for the day. The General rode up to them, and gave them what money he had in his pocket. At Caraballa Torta, in the middle of the night, I observed whole sections marching apparently fast asleep, and only awaking when the column halted by marching up against those in front of them.

At the bridge of Betanzos, the Engineer officer thought the match for exploding the mine had gone out. He went up to examine it, when it exploded, and blew him to atoms. When we drew near Corunna, as the ships had not come round from Vigo, a position was occupied about three miles in front of it, the left of which was good, but it sloped gradually down towards the right, where it was completely overlooked by the opposite heights above the village of Elvina.

A magazine containing nearly 4000 barrels of gunpowder was blown up there. It shook heaven and earth. It being a fine still morning, the vibration of the mist along the mountains was very beautiful, while a dense column of smoke ascended to a great height in the air.

The videttes of both armies seemed to think that the end of the world had arrived, and galloped off in opposite directions.

The night before the battle, the rattling of the French artillery getting into position, gave note of preparation. The battle itself has been so often described, that it is unnecessary to come over it again. Our battalion formed part of the reserve on the right and rear of the Army. We advanced up the hill, driving the enemy's skirmishers before us, but having very little ammunition, it was soon expended. When we were near the top of the hill, we came suddenly upon a considerable body of the enemy, standing in close column in a narrow valley, within fifty or sixty yards of us. They looked *shaky* and I believe very little would have sent them off, for I observed some of them pulling down a stone wall on their right to make an opening. Oh! for a few thousand rounds of ammunition, then! for notwithstanding the disasters of the retreat, we still mustered 700 men of the right sort. We had then got completely on the flank of the enemy, and had we got to the heights of Elvina, I think we should have peppered their hinder parts well.

As it was, the enemy finding our arms mute, became the assailants, and drove us down the hill faster than we went up.

At the foot of it I got into a garden, a complete *cul de sac,* open towards the enemy, and inclosed on the other sides by a high wall, which I clambered up with some difficulty. When I got to the top, I found Plunket behind me calling out for assistance, and as I had no desire to leave my poor friend to the tender mercies of his pursuers, I turned round, and made him hold up his rifle, which I caught by the muzzle, and while he held by the butt I dragged him to the top. We then descended, and the 52nd coming up to our support, drove back the enemy in their turn; but daylight and the battle were then near a close.

The Army retired during the night, and the rear guard entered Corunna about daybreak, where much confusion prevailed. Dragoons were shooting their horses on the beach, and wounded men creeping along on all fours to get on board, while some resolute Spaniards were beating up for recruits, sword in hand, to defend their city, and which they actually did for three days after we left it.

As we passed the glacis of the citadel the body of our Commander had just been committed to mother earth.

> "Lightly they'll talk of the spirit that's gone,
> And o'er his cold ashes upbraid him;
> But little he'll reck if they'll let him sleep on,
> In a grave where Britons have laid him."

I got on board a horse transport lying off the castle of Saint Antonio. There was no officer on board, but the non-commissioned officers were very kind to me and made me some coffee. The Admiral had been firing signals for some time, for the fleet to get under weigh, to which no attention was paid, until the French brought down some guns to the opposite side

107

of the bay. The second they fired killed a man in a boat alongside of us. Cut the cables was then the order of the day, and no fleet ever started more expeditiously. Unfortunately the vessel to windward of us drifted down upon us, hooked our main-yard, and as it was blowing fresh we both went upon the rocks, as did two or three more. I ran along the bowsprit and got into the next ship. She heeled over very much, and a boat from the Audacious coming under her quarter I let myself down into it, followed by others; the boat was very soon filled, and the officer shoved off to prevent being swamped. Numbers jumped into the sea, some of them got upon the rocks, while others were drowned. We then pulled for the Audacious, the only vessel remaining in the bay. The French had then turned their fire upon her, which she returned from her lower deck guns. They honoured our boat with a few shots, none of which took effect, although some of them came quite near enough to be agreeable, making the water fly to a great height in the air. Before we reached her the Audacious got under weigh, and anchored again outside, while the fleet, except the greater part of the line-of-battle ships, bore away for England. Next morning, a magazine was blown up in the town, to the west of which the enemy had advanced, while the embarkation of some of the troops remaining still continued from the rocks out of the town. When all were on board, the Ville de Paris stood out with 3200 men on board, and made a signal for relief. The whole then bore away.

Much has been said about the Corunna retreat. The situation in which Sir John Moore was placed was no doubt one of the greatest difficulty. Thwarted by traitors and false information, with an inexperienced army, staff, and commissariat, his situation required the utmost caution. The old maxim, *Nil mortuis nisi bonum,* is a good one, and in so gallant a soldier it is painful to censure any part of his proceedings. That he committed mistakes, however, I think his warmest admirers must admit. He always appeared to me as to want confidence in himself, and ill to bear responsibility. The public never gives a man credit for the possessing of these qualities, although so few possess them. The want of them has killed many of our statesmen; and the *Iron Duke* is certainly not a little indebted for his success in possessing them in so remarkable a degree. It certainly was an error to send the greater part of the artillery round by Madrid, where it narrowly escaped capture, as Sir John must have been aware of the road that Junot took to Lisbon. Still, however, his army was assembled on the plains of Leon in admirable order, 26,000 strong. The ill-judged advance to attack at Saldanha ruined it. He lost a week by that movement, which he never made up. Everything was hurry and confusion. Stores were destroyed, while the troops were starving; and none of the bridges were effectually blown up. Those of Lugo and Betanzos, in particular, if completely broken down, would have greatly retarded the enemy. Again, his separating his army, and sending part to Vigo, showed the enemy clearly that his intention was to embark. It has been urged that the advance of the British army prevented Napoleon from detaching a force to the south: but the same effect would have been produced had it not advanced; for Napoleon never put an enemy to the inconvenience of going in search of him. Both Corunna and Ferrol ought to have been put in a state of defence upon the landing of Sir D. Baird; for which there was ample time. It has been said that the Spaniards were jealous of the British occupying their strongholds; but we had possession of Corunna, and the troops of the Marquis of Romana, after the defeat of Reynosa, might have been thrown into Ferrol. That officer was one of the few Spanish chiefs cordially disposed to co-operate with the British. Neither of these are very strong places; but the French had no battering-train within three hundred miles of them, and the experience of all ages has shown how difficult it is to capture a place where supplies can be thrown in at pleasure during a siege.

Had these precautions been adopted, and Sir John Moore occupied the heights of Elvina with 26,000 men, it would have been very difficult for Soult to force him, and those heights might have been the lines of Torres Vedras.

Soult could not long have kept his force together, and must have carried on operations at a great disadvantage there, as he afterwards found to be the case, and evacuated that province at an early period of the war.

The Duke of Wellington seems to have been doubtful at one time if the northern frontier of Spain would not have afforded a preferable base of operations to Portugal. It certainly would have had great advantages in its vicinity to England, while the Asturian frontier is the most defensible in Spain.

Both Asturias and Gallicia are admirably adapted for a guerilla warfare. The people of England never seem to have been fully aware of the vast importance of this system, although it is well known that the French attribute the loss of Spain principally to it. Much might have been done in supplying them with proper arms and ammunition. The proper arm for them was a light fusil, weighing about 6lbs., such as is used by the smugglers in the South of Spain, where they form so numerous a body, and where they constitute so large a portion of the guerillas. In the *Sierra of Ronda* I have seen the bones of Frenchmen lying by the mountain tracks, where a single man had waited for a column, and having taken his shot, and killed his man, he was off. Any one who has ever pulled a trigger will at once perceive how ill adapted a bar of iron, yclept a British musket, is for such a system of warfare. Yet these muskets were sent out to Spain by the Ordnance Department during the war, by hundreds of thousands, at a vast expense to England, to be thrown away by the Spaniards the first convenient opportunity. Truly the Woolwich Mandarins have cost very dear to England.

After this Plunket and myself were a long time separated. I went on the Walcheren expedition, and afterwards to the south of Spain, while he went to Portugal. I was afterwards informed, however, that he was not idle; that he killed another General, and no doubt put his mark upon many others.

One day he happened to be trudging along the road, with a pig in a string behind him, when, as bad luck would have it, who should overtake him but Bob Craufurd. The salutation, as may be supposed, was not the most cordial.

"Where did you steal the pig, you plundering rascal ?" Tom, turning round to him with an air of surprise,—"What pig, Ginerl ?" "What pig! why, that pig you have got behind you, you villain you" Tom turning round to his friend, as if he had never seen him before,— "Well, I declare, Ginerl, some fellow, wanting to get me into trouble, has tied that *baste* to my cartouch box."

The General could contain his risible faculties no longer, stuck spurs into his horse and rode on.

When I returned to England I found Plunket swelled up like a beer barrel, and as yellow in the face as a guinea. Upon inquiring the cause of so strange a metamorphosis, I found that a French Dragoon had ridden over him and damaged his internals considerably. I thought it was all up with my poor friend; he recovered, however, and was soon as ready for the wars as ever. As he was then in a different battalion from me, I gave a Serjeant in exchange for him, and away we went, like the Knight of La Mancha, in search of adventures. We went first to Bilbao, and from thence to Passages. As we drew near St. Sebastian the wind died away, and the tide carried our ship within range of the guns of the fortress; but as the siege was then near a close, the Governor had no ammunition to spare for us. The island of Santa Clara was stormed that night, which had a beautiful effect from the sea. The day that we landed I visited the approaches and breaching batteries, and as a considerable number of volunteer stormers had arrived from the Light Division, I dined and passed the evening with the gallant fellows, then said adieu, pretty well aware that we should never all meet again.

Next day we had a long and fatiguing march to Vera, where we were at once informed that there would be a fight the following day; for it so happened that no detachment from England ever joined the regiment during the whole of the Peninsular war, that there was not a fight that day or the following one. Accordingly, next morning at daybreak, the alarm was sounded from the outposts, and upon looking out we saw about 24,000 men standing in close column opposite to us. Tents were immediately struck, and we stood to our arms to look out for squalls.

The enemy occupied the celebrated position of Vera, and the Light Division the ridge opposite to it on the south. The Bidassoa ran along our left, nearly due north, until it reaches the base of the hill of Vera, when it trends to the west. The bridge of Vera, across the Bidassoa, was also on our left, and a breastwork opposite to it on the left bank, completely commanding it. This breastwork was occupied by Longa's *bravos,* and had been erected when the relative position of the armies was different. By an unlucky oversight, it had not been levelled, nor the bridge broken down. Had that been done it might have changed the whole features of the campaign, and been productive of the most important consequences, as will presently appear.

Soult's manoeuvres were very beautiful, and it was some time before his plan of operations unfolded itself. His first movement was to send a body of troops across the river below the bend, which, taking the breastwork in reverse, drove the Spaniards before them, occupied it, and thus got the complete command of the bridge. The main body then filed off to its right, and moved on until we lost sight of it. It then appeared that the relief of St. Sebastian was his object. About 1000 or 1200 men were left in the position of Vera, who gave us an occasional shot during the whole day to distract our attention. In the afternoon a battalion passed the river, and marching along the left bank, almost within musket-shot of us, occupied the hill on our left, from which they shook their blanket at us, shouting most vociferously. They also brought a gun across the river, from which they fired some shots, and killed two or three men. We had also three men wounded from the bridge, all of which had to quit the field, at the distance of 1200 yards. This was the longest range at which I ever saw musketry take effect, and I afterwards ascertained it by taking a sketch of the ground.

In the afternoon a heavy firing was heard in the direction of St.Sebastian. The French had encountered the Spaniards, who fought most gallantly, the Duke being present, and after an obstinate conflict the enemy was repulsed at all points. In the evening the rain fell in torrents, which raised the river so as to render it impossible for them to recross it where they had passed it in the morning. The bridge of Vera was then their only alternative. They forced the passage next morning at three o'clock, when both our sentinels there fired, and gave the alarm. We had two companies on our side of the bridge behind the houses and stone walls in the neighbourhood of it, who immediately stood to their arms, and kept up an incessant fire upon the enemy the whole night. As soon as daylight appeared, the remainder of the battalion occupied a low ridge parallel to the river, so as to take them in flank on their march from the bridge to the town of Vera; and we gave them our last cartridge. Towards the close of the action the enemy opened two howitzers upon us from the hill of Vera, at a range of about 800 yards. But from the shortness of the range, and the softness of the ground, the shells sunk, and did no harm. The enemy commenced crossing the bridge at three, and continued doing so until about half past eight o'clock, A.M. It since appears the number that passed were between 12,000 and 14,000. Had the bridge been broken down, it is probable that the whole of these would have been made prisoners, for our army was so placed that they could hardly have escaped. They left seventy dead at the bridge; and we estimated their wounded at six or seven hundred. At the close of the action the valley was completely filled with smoke.

In the absence of the main body of the enemy, the position of Vera might easily have been forced and occupied by the Light Division, but General Skerritt, who commanded in the absence of Baron Alten, who had gone to witness the storming of St. Sebastian, did not think himself warranted in attempting it, as it might interfere with the Duke's operations.

Poor Sandy Campbell, a fine young Highlander who went out with me, whose career was to be so short, went into action for the first time under the auspices of Plunket, and never ceased talking afterwards of the way in which his instructor plied the rifle. Capt. Mac—, he of engineering celebrity, was sent to bury the dead. They were all stripped, —an operation at which the Spaniards were particularly expert. When he returned, he gave us an account of his operations. "There was an officer," said he, "who had a dam fine *soord*, which I wanted very much to get, but the fellow would not part with it. So I got a punch, and tried to open his fingers—still he would not part with it ; so I admired him so much for not parting with his *soord*, that I dug a grave for him, and buried him *soord* and all." This was probably the body of General Vandermaesen, who fell there.

After this, the enemy was for some time busily employed in fortifying his position, and in erecting huts for the winter. The Duke having resolved on forcing it, the point of attack assigned to our division was the hill of Vera—rather a tough job.

A battalion of ours drove in the enemy's skirmishers on the right, while our battalion and one of Caçadores did the same on the left. We then pushed on against the lower redoubt, and some got into the ditch, when I observed a French officer get up on the parapet, and kill a man of mine with a stone by fracturing his skull. Before he got down again, however, Dick Underhill put his mark upon him, and he fell lifeless into the ditch beside his victim.

The enemy made a desperate resistance, and we were in the act of recoiling, when the 52nd came on double quick to our support, and I can never forget the gallant bearing of that noble

115

regiment. When within fifty or sixty yards of the redoubt, the enemy evacuated it in a body, and a reinforcement, coming down the hill to their support, also thought it prudent to retire. Surely in a charge it is the countenance of the troops which produces the effect, and not the bit of iron yclept a bayonet. The 52nd then very prudently halted under the brow of the hill, while we filed a little to the left, and advanced under cover to within twenty yards of the upper entrenchments, the steepness of the ground affording cover at that short distance. A Serjeant, who put up his head to have a look, got a ball through it directly. We remained in that position for several hours, until our right brigade turned the enemy's works, and drove them out of them. Their left flank being turned, their right found it necessary to retire also, and as we were near neighbours, we had not far to travel, when we joined them company and helped them down the hill. A soldier of the 52nd who had joined us, was particularly industrious; he first shot one man, bayoneted a second, then, slipping his musket over his shoulder, and catching it by the muzzle, knocked the brains out of a third with the butt end of it. I rather think that he went through this exercise more than once. His Captain, R—, afterwards told me that he had the misfortune to be mad; but there certainly was method in his madness on this occasion.

Poor Sandy Campbell, who had behaved most gallantly, and was pushing on one of the foremost, was struck in the femoral artery by one of the last shots that was fired. He returned smiling, and said that he was wounded. Some of his brother officers, who at once saw the nature of the wound, laid him down on the ground, and tied a handkerchief round it, which they twisted with a ramrod; but the wound was so high up, that nothing could stay life's ebbing torrent. Plunket, who was much attached to him, notwithstanding the excitement of the moment

116

remained with him to the last; he then dug a grave for him with his sword, and consigned the body to its mother earth before he left it.

Colonel Colborne (now Lord Seaton) pushed on almost alone, and getting ahead of a body of the enemy, summoned them to lay down their arms, which they very politely did. Among the prisoners was a loquacious little Major, who had come a few days before with a flag of truce, and who strongly recommended us to try their hill, as they had tried ours unsuccessfully. The little man seemed considerably chopfallen. In this action the 9th French regiment was nearly destroyed; our battalion also suffered severely, our loss amounting to 7 officers and 98 men; one company of Caçadores had 15 killed. In riding over the ground three days afterwards, I found the Spaniards, particularly women, very busy in stripping the dead. I remonstrated with them on the indecency of their proceedings, and got a volley of slang for my pains. As I rode through the dead, I was horrified to see one body raise its arm and drop it again; I made the Spaniards raise him up, but he expired in doing so.

After this, Soult took up the line of the Nive, which he immediately set about fortifying with extraordinary vigour. The Duke remained inactive, awaiting the fall of Pampeluna, but that event had no sooner occurred than he resumed the offensive. The night before the battle of the Nivelle, the Light Division bivouacked behind a ridge of rocks, within musket-shot of the enemy's posts on La Petit Rhine, without being discovered. The enemy occupied that position, about a mile in front of their line, as an advanced post, in considerable force. Next morning at day-break, as soon as the signal was given (three cannon-shot at the centre) each column advanced to its point of attack. Ours being La Petite Rhine, our left brigade turned the enemy's right, where they had a strong breastwork built of stone; but so completely were they taken by surprise, that they had no time to occupy it, and we accordingly met with no resistance there. The 43rd, which attacked in front, met with more opposition, and suffered considerably. The enemy was soon driven down the hill, however, leaving all his tents standing.

This brought us in front of the hill on which the enemy's principal redoubt stood. The attack in the meantime was going on to our right for several miles. We had some skirmishing at the bottom of the hill, and a pretty smart cannonade was kept up from it. Clausel was very conspicuous in front of the great redoubt, riding a piebald horse, and galloping this way and that. Having expended his grape, I presume, he fired a round of dollars at us, rather an unusual instance of patriotism in the great nation.

The division on our right having broken through the enemy's line, he retired opposite to us, leaving the garrison in the great redoubt to its fate. In this state of things, the 52nd was ordered to storm the great redoubt,—an order which no one seems ever to have acknowledged; and in that mad attempt lost 200 men, and this at a time when the garrison was completely isolated.

In the hottest of the fire, and when the men were falling fast, a hare started from the bushes under their feet, at which our mad friend of Vera took a cool shot as she ran away. The garrison was summoned immediately after, and laid down their arms. It consisted of the 88th Regiment, or as our soldiers called them, "the French Connaught Rangers," and queer-looking fellows they were: their beards were plaited like a horse's mane, with a piece of lead at the end of it.

The army then advanced to the vicinity of Bayonne, where it remained during the winter; that season, however, did not pass over quietly. The Duke having resolved to blockade Bayonne on our right, between the Nive and the Adour, the left of the army made a feint, to draw the enemy's attention that way, while General Hill crossed the Nive, and occupied the heights above Bayonne. The movement succeeded perfectly, although the *diversion*, as it is termed, cost us 500 men. At first our division was but slightly engaged, except the 43rd, which suffered considerably in attacking a fortified house; our battalion had some slight skirmishing at long shots. Plunket and a few men being sent in front, a French officer got up on the top of a bank, apparently as a sort of bravado, where he stood a long time, Plunket firing at him all the while, about a range of 500 yards. At last, he appeared to us to leap down, but presently after we saw him carried off in a blanket. A few more men were then sent down to place themselves on the left of the skirmishers, but they returned shortly after; and upon being asked the reason, one of them replied, "Plunket, Sir, says, he'll be — if any man shall go before him." The apology was admitted. We then advanced, and the skirmishing was sharp. Plunket was by the side of a road leading towards the enemy, behind a thorn bush; but of the two men who were with him, one of them was severely wounded, and the other killed. I called to him to come over to a cross-road where I was; but he coolly replied, reloading his rifle, "I must stop here, Sir, to keep a look-out," We then advanced to the heights on the west of Bayonne; and after exchanging a few cannon-shot with the enemy, retired in the night to our cantonments, which we reached next morning, after a dreary march, the rain falling in torrents.

We were hardly warm in our beds, when the alarm was given of the enemy's advance. Soult finding himself hemmed in, made a countermovement to that of the Duke, by threatening our left, and draw our force that way, to enable him to disengage his left.

His first attack was on the church of Arcanyuse, where he was repulsed by our gallant friends the 43rd, under the Historian. After our brigade came up on their left, we had some skirmishing, which ceased early in the day, except on our left, where the Portuguese and French amused themselves by chasing each other backwards and forwards across the plain during the day, amid much noise, and no trifling expenditure of gunpowder. Trade being slack in front of us, Plunket went down with another man in the afternoon to have a lark with the Portuguese. They espied two Frenchmen carrying a pig across a field, at which they fired, and shot them both. The object then was, to get possession of the prize; and for that purpose, the manoeuvres of General Plunket and his army were rather amusing; such marching and countermarching—such flank movements—and such creeping upon all fours; Arthur himself never manoeuvred better. The French were equally expert on their side, and between the two the prize remained unclaimed.

As the weather was very cold, we sent for our tents, and pitched them, although very near the enemy, for the division was so expert in packing, that a quarter of an hour, was sufficient for that purpose at any time. As I lay in my tent, the gossip went on around the watchfire as usual; for the fellows seemed never to sleep, and their good humour never left them. Those men of iron, those hearts of steel, we shall never see their like again! they talked of home and friends with much good feeling: they talked of the loss of their comrades, and they talked of the loss of the pig.

"Well," said one, "when Tom Turtle was hit, he was as well covered as any man could be."

"I hardly think so," said another; "for you know he was killed."

"Well, *barrin'* a bit of his head, it -was as I say."

"Plunket," said another, "I'm as good a soldier as you are."

"You a soldier!" was the reply; "you haven't the *makins* of a soldier in you; you're a poor man, Sir!"

Plunket then gave them a dissertation on skirmishing, and no tactician ever did it better. He ended by telling them, "above all things, beware of *a flankin'* fire, boys; for if they bring a flankin' fire upon you, three men will drive a thousand!"

Soult then directed his attacks along the ridge parallel to our front, where there was hard fighting for three days. He then retired his troops through Bayonne in the night, and attacked Hill next morning, when a fierce conflict ensued, in which he was completely defeated.